IMPERIAL YOUTH REVIEW

THE SEX ISSUE

T0315706

EDITED BY
CHRIS KELSO AND GARRETT COOK

Published by
Dog Horn Publishing
45 Monk Ings, Birstall, Batley WF17 9HU
United Kingdom
doghornpublishing.com
sales@doghornpublishing.com

Edited by
Chris Kelso and Garrett Cook

ISBN 978-1-907133-91-6

Cover design by
Adam Lowe

Typesetting by
Jonathan Penton

UK Distribution: NBN Internationals
10 Thornbury Road, Plymouth, PL6 7PP, United Kingdom
orders@centralbooks.com
Telephone:+44 (0) 1752 202301
Email: cservs@nbninternational.com

Overseas Distribution: Printondemand-worldwide.com
9 Culley Court, Orton Southgate, Peterborough, PE2 6XD, United Kingdom
Telephone: 01733 237867
Email: info@printondemand-worldwide.com

IMPERIAL YOUTH REVIEW

THE SEX ISSUE

INTRODUCTION
by Garrett Cook

This started as a stupid pun. As a Bizarro author, I am not altogether immune to the desire to take something that looks like a fucking joke too far, dangerously far, tase him and drag off his ass far, far far far too fucking far. It started as a pun inspired by *Giantsized Man Thing*, the Seymour Butts of 70s comic titles. I did want to do an issue focused on sex because it was something I wanted to rediscover in myself and in the world. I had just ended a relationship when IYR first came into being and I was living in Boston and I was confused. I was scared that I would never touch a woman again. I was scared that I would never want to.

Through the history of this issue, the two years I spent making this the biggest, best new issue I could, to prove that not only can we survive but we can thrive, my life and love changed. I did fall in love again. And again. And Christ Almighty, I will fall in love again. It's been important for me to put together a portrait of sexuality that looks at it from various angles, from the exaltation in love, to slutshaming, to BDSM, passion, triumph, tragedy, sex toys and despair. This is what love and connection look like.

Sex is connection. You can't tell anybody shit about love until you've learned to connect again. And the only way to connect is by connecting. It's that simple. It's that complicated. In these pages, I have work by lovers, a brother, a surrogate mother, a sister, a captivating shadow dancing outside my periphery, by people whose wisdom, strength and sensuality have moved me and reminded me why I do what I do, work by students, whose work I have had to connect with, by a couple whose example of love reminds me to call nothing less love And oh yeah, also William Burroughs. Everything in here is something that I have found connection with.

It took me two years to bring this together and now it's together. We don't have long in this world and without the force, the vitality, the heat of human connection, it becomes Hell. We all have issues, some bigger than others. Here's one of them.

INTRODUCTION
by Chris Kelso

It's funny...

I am a late-comer to sex. In fact, I didn't lose my virginity till I was 17 years old – and it'd be another year later until I'd experience it again! It does seem strange that I should be a part of a magazine themed around sex. I always appreciated the culture and cartoons present within the pages of Playboy and Hustler mind you. I can't shake the feeling that I don't belong.

But then again… I do LOVE sex. It makes sense that my literary endeavours should reflect my own ideologies and subjects of interest – sex being, probably, at the apex of my various preoccupations! Fuck it. Let's do this! Let's have a sex issue edited by Garrett Cook and…Chris Kelso. Yes, it's not so unbelievable. Is it? No, exactly! Shut up you!

In the same fashion as those early lifestyle magazines, here are a bunch of people with much vaster intellect and greater sexual prowess than I could ever hope to achieve for you to enjoy.

Enjoy its sweat, enjoy its humour, enjoy it's deviancy. Enjoy it, like me, vicariously…

A note from Garrett Cook:
Chris Kelso is handsome as fuck and his accent is adorable. He is probably having sex right now.

TABLE OF CONTENTS

UNFROSTED

Now it is beginning and nobody knew it.
The auto accident continued to repeat itself
In the brochure and flowers were shaking the air
For more moonlight. The demonstration of sleep
Had made him beautiful. A bibliography was offered.
The poem found its way into our headaches. In the boat
House we committed the action of sodomy
To drift across the floor
Boards and think of the bird who would not stay.
But the boat was firmly moored to the pier in need of repair.
What were we to be included into?
And did it rise into the negative sky
Line?? Everything else floats in its own time
Machine. Now I am coming in and out of you
In dreams of corduroy. The clouds
Carefully included you into focus
Geared up for the big race. But who recovers
From the weight of the tornado fiend?
Everything was continuing continuing:
Headlights plunging into the dark
Farther ahead was a bridge through which
There were the remains of ~~transparent~~ miles of
~~Railroad.~~ Collisions we have missed (one line)
~~indicated by several runs~~
Markings that were no longer specific.
But what here of us they thought heard
Into our sleekest parts and the dream of
The dashboard, the continuing destination that was not theirs?
Sparks were coming from my hair. His name is John.
But now his name is no longer John,
Or was it Freddy who exists in the clouds
In disguise yearning for the point from which
He took off, as if dying depended
On height and repetition in the fabulous dry
Turmoil of a long afternoon these sensations are making on him.
This keeps happening only once without encouragement.
Though it is only real to rise onto another surrender of air,
Leaving us at that and the body that was not fractured nor bruised.

MEDITATIONS

Soon it will rain
Beside the pillow
Case. Did anyone listen
Into it? It is midday.

He compulsively wrote,
"Sometimes the sky is gr...
Then another yellow shad...
Is covered in the square...

Already it is late
Afternoon. What is...
Difficult is crossed out...
A hand is in the brochure...

On the street a news
Paper is covered with w...
Toward the sides of
A tense day.

Nobody is driving here.
The clouds are catching...
To us and now the birds...
Are trying to come, too.

Gerard Malanga

THE BLUE DRESS

It happens several times a year
Everywhere inside the grounds.
Yesterday it was hectic and muddy.
"I can't help what you say," he said.
Alas, wisdom is the only gift I can receive.
Later, probably fearing they might report him,
He ordered them away. Next day
They quietly climbed the bluff behind the cave.

At sea the ship is out at sea.
It was in such earthly terms, it seemed.
I think (sic) we are going to get even
More involved. The book I need to
Borrow it immediately. Aren't we charged
In the month of the ranch-hand already?
Somehow it seems sufficient to know everything.

The name Guillaume Apollinaire has reached my ears.
Across the street a girl goes away from me.
It happens several times a year.
Any look we had taken before is a lost look.
And now the cars are moving. We have entered
A new green country where suspicion
Is one of us instead of him.

I understand, all the same, that the limousine
Has taken me into a year that is new and photogenic.
And now the cars are moving. Someone sees a face,
Recalls a "wanted" poster-- another criminal
Is brought to justice. Across the street a girl,
In the likeable image of Ivy Nicholson,
Walks away from me, tall, slimmer and fair-complexioned.

c/o Andy Warhol
1342 Lexington Avenue
New York City, New York
16 Dec 64

Dear Charles Plymell:
Annie has told me that you have taken three of
my poems for NOW. I'm very honored to be in your
magazine. I liked the last issue very, very much.

I presume you have taken "Windshield", "Negotiation"
and "The Blue Dress". There are two revisions in
"Windshield" as follows:

     "Collisions we have missed indicated by severed
     road"

is all on one line, and fifth line from the bottom
should read

     "On repitition and height in the fabulous dry"

I believe the word "fractured" in the last line was
misspelled, but maybe not.

Hope to hear from you soon. Allen and Peter send
their best.

                              Adios,
                              Gerard

Gerard Malanga

Gerard Malanga

WINDSHIELD
by Gerard Malanga

Now it is the beginning and nobody knew it.
The auto accident continued to repeat itself
In the brochure and flowers were checking the air
For more sunlight. The demonstration of sleep
Had made him beautiful. A bibliography was offered.
The poem found its way into our headaches. In the boat
House we committed the action of sodomy
To drift across the floor
Boards and think of the bird who would not stay.
But the boat was firmly secured to the pier in need of repair.
What were we to be included into?
And did it rise into the negative sky
Line?? Everything else floats in its own time
Machine. Now I am coming in and out of you
In dreams of corduroy. The clouds
Carefully included you into focus
Geared up for the big race. But who recovers
From the weight of the tornado fiend?
Everything was continuing continuing:
Headlights plunging into the dark
Further ahead was a bridge through which
There were the remains of
Miles of collisions we have missed indicated by several road
Markings that were no longer specific.
But what here of we they thought heard
Into our sleekest parts and the dream of
The dashboard, the continuing destination that was not theirs?
Sparks were coming from my hair. His name is John.
But now his name is no longer John,
Or was it Freddy who exists in the clouds

In disguise yearning for the point from which
He took off, as if dying depended
On height and repetition in the fabulous dry
Turmoil of a long afternoon these sensations are making on him.
This keeps happening only once without encouragement,
Though it is only real to rise onto another surrender of air,
Leaving me at that and the body that was not fractured nor bruised.

Gerard Joseph Malanga *is an American-Italian poet, photographer, filmmaker, curator and archivist.*

NEGOTIATIONS
by Gerard Malanga

Soon it will rain
Beside the pillow
Case. Did anyone listen
Into it? It is midday.

He compulsively wrote,
"Sometimes the sky is grey."
Then another yellow sheet
Is covered in the square.

Already it is late
Afternoon. What is
Difficult is crossed out.
A hand is in the brochure.

On the street a news
Paper is covered with words
Toward the close of
A tense day.

Nobody is driving here.
The clouds are catching on
To us and now the birds
Are trying to come, too.

THE BLUE DRESS
by Gerard Malanga

It happens several times a year
Everywhere inside the grounds.
Yesterday it was hectic and muddy.
"I can't help what you say," he said.
Alas, wisdom is the only gift I can receive.
Later, probably fearing they might report him,
He ordered them away. Next day
They quietly climbed the bluff behind the cave.

At sea the ship is out at sea.
It was in such earthly terms, it seemed.
I think (sic) we are going to get even
More involved. The book I need to
Borrow it immediately. Aren't we charged
In the month of the ranch-hand already?
Somehow it seems sufficient to know everything.

The name Guillaume Apollinaire has reached my ears.
Across the street a girl goes away from me.
It happens several times a year.
Any look we had taken before now is a last look.
And now the cars are moving. We have entered
A new green country where suspicion
Is one of us instead of him.

I understand, all the same, that the limousine
Has taken me into a year that is new and photogenic.
And now the cars are moving. Someone sees a face,
Recalls a "wanted" poster—another criminal
Is brought to justice. Across the street a girl,
In the likeable image of Ivy Nicholson,
Walks away from me, tall, slender, and pale-complexioned.

GILDENPELT AND FORBEARANCE
by Colette Torrez

Liberty Stalwart sauntered with a slow sway, brazenly bare-assed (most of her naked), as she strolled from the greenhouse under its canopy of stars (their part of the Ship was nightside at this hour), back to the Stalwarts' livingpod. She cradled a mass of chrysanthemums. Fluffy heads of pale-green petals nodded over slender necks of electric lilac, in kaleidoscopic contrast to her own fairly-rare phenotype: green-blue eyes, golden hair, ebony skin. Her parents had been geneticists. (When she'd turned thirteen, she had sulked for half a year at them for not giving her turquoise hair to match her eyes, unhappy that she was tri-color.) Regulations required rayscreen creams or suit-ups when exposed to space radiation – or worse, the sun – but she defied this all the time, counting on her extra melanin for protection. She hated changing into clothes just to check on the garden, only to have to shed them to return to the comfort of customary skin when in-pod again.

The Stalwarts possessed the only personal lawn and greenhouse on the Station. Unlike any of their Shipscomrades' apartments, their own livingpod extended a bit from the outermost ring of quarters in a narrow peninsula that benefitted from a small portion of sunlight that the food and oxygen gardens received from the overhead transparent segment of the Ship, open to the sun for a third of every 72-hour rotation. It was not an Earth-Standard exposure, and the crops had been finessed to thrive under this particular cycle. Liberty Stalwart was the Ship's plant geneticist, and a second-generation Spacer; she had applied for a grant to see if the Ship could profit from the exotic floral market as well, and had secured permission and funding. It helped that their Station exported more food and oxygen than it consumed. She had snuck in a lawn (as a side experiment) for

Dunn's pleasure as well; her husband had been born planetside, and missed greenery. Of course she had then been obliged to request a livingpod extension as well, to keep an eye on the experiment.

As Liberty waltzed into their homepod with her armful of blooms, a sharp odor wafted her way: that strongest of male scents, the one that arose from heavy exertion. The skunky pheromones instantly overpowered the faint perfume of the flowers. Dunn must have just returned to their quarters, and had obviously not yet washed. The flowers had delighted her, but the smell that announced her husband reminded her more charmingly of their bedroom acrobatics.

As he emerged, glistening and nude, at the far end of the hall, she glanced first at her husband's upper lip, then past his long nose to the dark brow. Might it be the first glimmer of fear beading there, and not only the dew of his work-out? She stared a few moments longer, and sniffed: no, no smell of panic. It had only been her (shameful) hope that nerve would betray itself somehow on his large, competent body. (To keep company with her own rising alarm.) But only the traces of physical labor were cause for the rills gleaming down his chest, the swamp at armpit and pubic hair. Dunn caught her gaze.

"A little on edge, are we, GildenPelt?" he guessed. It was his pet name for her; on Ship, they were a minority of two in their cultivation of certain areas of body-hair. Most Shipscomrades chose permanent depilation, some completely, flaunting bald heads.

He had a surprisingly soft voice for such a strapping man. She suspected he'd cultivated that gentleness when his voice first broke sometime in secondary tech; he disliked intimidating people, and his height and breadth by themselves were sufficient to dominate without his even wishing it. Only when he sang, or the rarer times he'd lost his temper, had she occasion to hear his rather thrilling *basso profundo* unchecked.

"Who, me?" she mocked herself. She busied her eyes and hands with sculpting the chrysanthemums she had rearranged all morning, their pale purple leaves wilting a little under all the handling. She pinched off the browning parts, refreshing the bouquet back to its original intensity.

Dunn had spent his day mowing the lawn with an antique (manual!) machine.

They both enjoyed their little anachronisms. She arranged flowers. Dunn claimed mowing the lawn re-connected him to the actual Earth, and re-enacting ancestral endeavors was a more fulfilling way to achieve peak physical condition than using the electric-stims and high-G force exercises of the Station's gymnasium could ever be.

The bragging rights inherent in meriting a permit to grow *his* lawn and *her* flowers was never mentioned between them. Their unspoken complicity of shared values and aesthetics was one of the many ways they complemented each other.

Take their quarters and its rare open greenspace surrounding it: When she'd learned of the grant's award, along with its unprecedented perquisites, she and Dunn had immediately sent out a Ship-wide communication, offering their livingpod as guestquarters to any off-Station visitors. Their text explained their surprise at the conditions the grant imposed on them (of course, had anyone read her application, they would have been not as amazed), how gratified they were at the honor, how selfish they would feel if they didn't share it to benefit their Shipscomrades. Though many were jealous, all admitted that the Stalwarts played well with others. (And more privately, how well they played The Game.)

Requests – and their denial – were part of the public record. Both she and Dunn eschewed looking...grasping. It was enough to modestly murmur "Thank you" when they shared the flowers of their labors and privileges. It was enough to be the cause of that sigh of dissatisfaction when other couples regarded their own less auspicious choices.

And so it became their habit to host off-Station travelers roughly once every Earth-standard month, or sometimes only every other.

They delighted in the reciprocal invitations they piled up, the ever-expanding network of cosmopolitan friends and contacts, and – not least – the social merit they accumulated by extending themselves to the Station's visitors. To their Shipscomrades, the lawned and flowered setting of their unique and private quarter seemed thus somewhat fair recompense for the disruption their private life occasionally experienced.

In fact, they constituted one type of model mated pair that Stations throughout the galaxy sought: hard-working, high-achieving, outgoing, attractive, ambitious but mindful of group dynamics, adventurous but stable, and mostly monogamous, but discreet and non-disruptive when not. With time-eating hobbies. In short, the Stalwarts were a credit to the Inter-Galactic Spirit of the times. Their little conceits and house-proudness were seen as harmless vanities that in fact attached them ever more tightly to the life of the Station.

"Me, nervous?" she asked again.

Dunn's smile met hers, the first moment of calm she'd enjoyed in a day of hectic and unnecessary re-decorating, flower-arranging, and ordering and then re-ordering from the serbots.

"They're just people, Liberty," he said, caressing her cheek, then one bared breast. It was plumped up and more jutting than usual due to late-twentieth-century red plush pads glued on to the undersides of her breasts. They had come with a brassiere, but she found wearing that as well made her sweat. Such items had cost a pretty credit.

"Really big, furry, fanged people," she countered.

Dunn suddenly bared his teeth in an exuberant grin.

"Big furry fanged people who speak Galactic!" he crowed. "And who have agreed to be *our* guests!"

His reminder of the reason she was preparing for invasion dissipated the rest of her anxieties.

"Who *almost* speak Galactic!" she laughed back. Suddenly a new worry dawned. "Dunn – what if they're allergic to chrysanthemums?" she worried. Some of their own species were, mostly Planetsiders. She dried her hands on her apron, her only other attire. It was made of a loose weave of gauze, almost transparent, and through which some of her golden pubic hair spiraled. She caught Dunn looking at her curls there.

"Oh, GildenPelt!" Using her private pussy-name again, Dunn's teasing exasperation held a sly note. He came closer, locked his hands behind her neck, and brought her face to within an inch of his. "I can think of something else to keep you busy for the next two hours till they come."

He stretched his head to hers and caught her lower lip in a strong, gentle bite. He stank excitingly of his labors on their lawn. She mewled in consent as her thighs parted to allow his exploring fingers access to her suddenly slick lower lips. His bobbing, purpling penis ruched up the antique ruffles of the apron. He nosed it with his gaping-eyed head.

"Almost silky enough stuff..." he teased, then brought the smooth head down a bit to rub against her silkier blonde pelt, and then knock at her pussy's door, the nerve center's doorbell of clitoris. Bump...bump... bump...he knocked.

"Eeeooa, aah" was her bell's carolling through both sets of lips.

"May I come in?"

"Yes!" she called as he entered. Then they both became less polite as she shimmied backward, keeping him in till her ass smacked against a wall to prop them up. Not too difficult to manage in low gravity, but just enough gravity to end up, after 10 minutes, coupling on the floor. Just enough gravity in their Station to feel... each....thrust...with gravity's resistance. Gravity's insistence.

One of the major benefits of living on a Station and not Earthside: low-g made *many* more positions possible.

--o0O0o--

That the Bears (so Liberty called them) were arriving was due as much to serendipity as design.

Their open Net to other worlds and Stations had led to being hailed by the Grstl'k's on the strength of a common houseguest, Vledjan in origin, who in fact they had thought rather churlish at visit's end, 'though they'd strained their imaginations to please him.

One day their Library screen had blared at them: "WE ARE RECOMMENDED VIA OUR MUTUAL COUSIN HIS WORSHIP GARL KRBGRS HAILS OF VLEDJ. SEE: EMINENT DOMAIN PRECEDENTS" was their puzzling introduction to the Bears, the first of many such correspondences.

"I thought that Vledjan's family name was *Crabgrass*," she'd mused a month ago. "And didn't we call him dear Karl, or was it

Growl? Perhaps he took insult…" Well, he'd evidently thought well enough of them to have passed on their heartfelt *"Please*, do tell your *friends* to look us up if ever they're in the neighborhood!"

In fact, further (confusing) conversations in mangled Galactic had established the Bears' intimate friendship with Garl Krbgrs, and the contagious enthusiasm for visiting the Stalwarts with which he had infected them.

The Stalwarts corresponded back: "Our home is your home. Please come any time."

The Bears accepted, the intergalactic channel spitting out "SUCH AN HONOR INVITATION WE HAVE RARELY HAD! TWO CYCLES FROM NOW FOR 2 NIGHTS MUTUALLY TOLERATE?" The Stalwarts were flattered.

And what a coup! To host such exotics! Little was known of the society of Krnnyr, a species only recently encountered in the vast intergalactic oceans of spacetime. Friendly, eager for trade, with a liberal religious tradition; so new to humankind, their respective planets' Nets had not yet plumbed each other's languages well enough to insta-translate. Clever Bears, to learn sufficient – if flawed – Trade Galactic, beating both worlds' own AI's (AI's being notable sticklers for accuracy over speed).

Dunn and Liberty combed the Library for every gleaning of their anticipated guests. "Grstl'k" was their visitors' clan/phenotype name; their species proudly interbred to stand out from fellow clans on their world. Only immediate offspring were taboo; siblings mated. Yet not a clan was xenophobic; they had commingled socially for centuries on their planets, with no wars, and were as eager as they were surprised to encounter other intelligent species.

The Grstl'k clan members were, in averaging 2.4 meters height, shorter but somewhat more muscular than their fellow clans. Bred for a silver-tinged sherry-brown all-over pelt, with large, close-set eyes of matching color, and with snouted nose and jaws (and, my! those jaws were large, and those fangs both large and pointed!), they most resembled the zoo-preserved Kodiak bear in the blurred repro-vizzies Liberty and Dunn diligently pored over.

And they were nearly here!

"Any minute now!" Liberty sang out gaily. Her resurgent mental anxieties were now only piquant, modified as they were by after-love lassitude. (How clever and considerate her husband was!)

They had dressed up for the occasion; that is, they were dressed at all. Vaunting antiques they were usually too well-mannered to parade before their less-fortunate – and admit it, less tasteful – Shipscomrades, they shrugged happily at the Bears' virgin social understanding of clothing – its significance and deconstruction – and "reached for outer orbit".

Her purple stretch velvet blouse was cut low and ended in v-shaped points front and back to delineate her waist. (Antique shop during a stopover on Cosk 7.) The skirt it was draped over was ankle length and of transparent ruffled gauze, much like the apron she'd worn earlier. Quite happy with the earlier effect the apron's fabric had aroused in Dunn, she deliberately pulled skinny tufts of her ornamental pubic hairs through the skirt's airy weave, to spring out in an artful burst of pale blonde coils.

She teetered a bit in thigh-high boots of silver/black plastic "Thai-Shantung" (whatever the Galaxy *that* was). They were wonderfully visible through the skirt. She hoped Bears could appreciate the artistry of opaque top contrasting with transparent bottom. Dressing was so much more effort than nudity, but she prided herself on those efforts that differentiated her from the rest of the Ship.

Dunn sported pleathern brown-silver tunic and tights. The tunic was cut in front in a "V" that reached his navel. They had gambled on his abundant chestnut hair pleasing the Bears' aesthetic, as closely matching in color their own fur. Her own blue-eyed, blonde-haired, black-skinned charms (thanks to her talented parents' finesse in juggling phenotypes) did not, perhaps regrettably, match them in any wise. Hence such care for her attire.

They had deliberated over cosmetiks, rejecting complex or all-over patterns, as they'd no doubt prove confusing to a species that had never seen them unembellished. Liberty and Dunn had both brushed up their brows and lashes with a little shine, and had stained their lips for emphasis. They had decided to allow Liberty the one amusement of a blue-green fluorescing painted curlicue that swung over and around the left eye alone, to clue in the Bears to make-up's frivolity. It glowed iridescent against her ebony brow, and picked up the turquoise of her eyes.

They gazed at each other in admiration. Her pussy gave a further little flutter at his regard.

"We're…we're…," he sought for the historic animal: "Peacocks!"

"Peacocks!" Liberty echoed him in perfect comprehension. They'd pulled up a documusement two years before, on Ostentatious Ornamentation, Natural and Found. "…Like moons of Kleptrex!"

Dunn winked at her as their built-in-obsolescent, every-year-replaced, up-to-the-minute circa 1976 doorbell rang. It whistled "Dixie".

"They come!" they said in unison, as she did again. Dunn didn't notice. He was springing towards the door.

~~-o0O0o-~~

A pair of shaggy jaws opened in giant, toothed smiles just over half a meter above them. In antiquarian terms, they were 8 feet tall, give or take a few inches more to the larger. The larger one rumbled. Liberty repressed the urge to shrink back.

"GREETINGS!" this larger one roared at her, bending at the waist to confront her eye to eye. Its large eyes were intelligent and beautiful, dark as brandy, with little white, and black-purple ovoid pupils.

"Welcome, Grstl'k ambassador," she braved back, relieved to note her voice's timbre held steady. "I am Liberty, the female." She offered her hand. It was engulfed in dry-palmed, large furred paws; no, the six long, furred fingers made them hands, she decided. Just different, decidedly large hands. They warmed her cooler ones.

Out of the corner of her eye, she noted Dunn greeting the other Bear. His feet dangled, toes skimming the floor, encircled by a fur vise that gripped him under his armpits. He swayed like a dress she might hold before her, to gauge its effect in a mirror, before trying on. She had never before seen him physically helpless. This frightened her. It even excited her.

Before she could puzzle out why, her own creature offered its name.

"LIBRRTEEhuh! CALL ME THE BG'RBPLEEK," it offered. So, this was the female, evidently first cousin to the male (the "Lee", as the Library had lectured), and in estrus (the "K" at the end, per the same source).

Bg'rbpleek was now dangling her as the smaller male had dangled Dunn; it felt almost safe, as if she were the larger SheBear's doll, but its hair tickled the naked tops of her breasts.

Abruptly, the pressure beneath her arms extended to her back, squashing both of her breasts into fuller globes bulging like two moons over her ribs, as the SheBear pressed Liberty to her massive chest in a torso-to-torso embrace. The creature's fur pricked sharply into all her exposed skin. The leathery bulb of its nose snuffled along her hairline; blew warm in her right ear like a playplanet's jasmine-scented night breeze; inhaled sharply – the pressure displacement in her ears making her suddenly queasy – and continued to snuffle and sniff like a wine connoisseur along Liberty's nose, mouth and chin; and then quickly and surprisingly, in the crevice between her breasts. Its softer, downy belly fur massed through the stuff of her skirt, to intermesh with her own pubic fur, whose curlier texture sprang to tug at it like an antiquarian Velcro seam. Her hairs down there were ensnared and tugged by the greater volume of the SheBear's fur. The sensation was…odd.

Then Liberty was on her feet again, given back to herself. Just in time, she remembered from her research to offer the Grstl'k Bg'rbpleek (unpronounceable!) corresponding facts about herself, and an offer of hospitality.

"Please follow me and sit down! My home is your home! Know that my husband and I are mated but of unknown consanguine relationship. Bigger-baleek…" (well, she'd tried) "I ovulate any time within the next 2 days but will negate this fertility. Cheese and wine?"

"PLEASE! PLEASE! PLEASE! YES!" rumbled SheBear. "I speak more softly your little drums in ears not to drown. I read so. KSF'NGR!" she bellowed to the other beast. "MORE QUIET POOR HUMANS REMEMBER!" The din to Liberty's left quieted. SheBear continued conversationally, "So it is confirmed as we researched: Earth origins beyond two generations randomize again?! Yet such FINE CREATURES!! Oh, sorry."

SheBear took Liberty's chin in her paw as she descended into a chair opposite Liberty's.

"My name is dif'cult for you in Galactic yes? You say in four sounds not two! HA HA HA! Then call me Bg'r you can say yes?"

"Yes, thank you – Bigger." Liberty clapped, and a serbot tray floated in with one crystal flask, four delicate glasses, three cheeses, and various breads. At her wave, it hovered before Bigger. "Brandy? Or…? " They had learned that Bears like strong flavors.

Bigger grabbed the carafe by its throat and drained it. Liberty leaned forward in alarm that her guest might have no inkling of its potency. Not to fret. Bigger leaned forward in response to breathe brandy fumes at her.

"ARGGH! GOOD! – Oh, sorry, quiet voice to use. SUCH nice fire drinks like on Krnnyr. Intoxicates also hallucinogenic? Aphrodisiac? Mutagenic?"

"Er, no. Just high alcohol content, I'm afraid." Nonplussed, she clapped once to attract a new serbot. "Three more bulbs of brandy." (They'd only the one antique vessel.) "On three separate trayfloats. Double the cheese on each one." She clapped again to end the order.

She desperately tried to avoid catching Dunn's eye in case she were to break out into nervous giggles, but she did anyway, little champagne bubbles of hysterical terror. Bigger barked along with her.

They both turned to Dunn and the male Bear. The smaller of the Bears, the male was at least two heads higher than Dunn, and half again as wide. Bigger's mate smiled, beaming his eyes right into hers. Etiquette between same-sex members had been served; now it was time for their introductions all around.

"KSF'NGR, LIBRRTEEhuh is good material KLEEK woman for you to MEET," she roared at her mate.

"DUNN IS FOR YOU!" her mate roared back.

Even Dunn jumped. Liberty and he traded slanting glances, then Liberty smiled calmingly and he gave her the same smile back.

Liberty hoped to act her next part correctly.

"Dunn, I'm very pleased for you to meet Bigger." She reached across their plush chairs to take her spouse's suddenly frail-seeming hand. She placed it in Bigger's fur muff. The Library had mentioned this bit of social anthropology thoroughly, 'though it was clear by now to them how much it had omitted, or had not yet unearthed about the Krnnyr. (They could contribute footnotes! even articles! with attributions.)

"Bigger, may I introduce my husband Dunn," she finished, just as Bigger bounded up more nimbly than she had imagined possible. Her heart pounding, she imagined going through the Bear-hug hold-up-and-sniff routine all over again in the next few seconds with HeBear, as Dunn was enduring or enjoying his present subjection to Bigger's attention.

The she-giant released him more slowly than she had Liberty, so that Dunn slid down the front of her body while still held tightly. His tunic rode up to his armpits. Liberty could see his abdominal and chest hairs tickle against the SheBear's. And when he was back on his feet again, saw more: his tunic still high up his stomach, she saw the unmistakable outline of an emergingly-larger volume of excited Dunn. This frisson had stimulated him? she pondered, not for long.

Already, Bigger had growled permission for her mate Fangor (as the Bears had amended his name for her use) to meet Liberty. She turned just in time to catch bright brown eyes and huge fanged grin. Then he pounced on her. A tiny shriek escaped her.

She was aloft again. As he snuffled her, his teeth looked even larger than his wife's, in a larger jaw. Up close, at almost 2 ⅓ meters, he certainly didn't feel any smaller than his mate. They were both just TOO LARGE. She immediately was ashamed of her thought.

He lunged at her neck. A single tear of piss stung her labia. She clenched her vaginal muscles hard to turn her bladder off. Fangor abruptly shot his nose downward and lifted her belly past his brow. His warm breath, felt in little bursts as he sniffed her crotch, made her spine crawl. His huge hairy elbows tickled the cheeks of her ass in this new position, and the hollows of her underarms ached where his great hands now dangled her. Over his head she saw SheBear and Dunn grinning at her. Weakly she grinned back.

Fangor gently slipped her down a bit, his arms circling her until he was supporting her, his hands slung interwoven underneath her ass, and their eyes again on a level.

"I provoked fear I smell," he whispered. "I very sorry am, littler Librr-tee-huh."

She gazed back into his intent eyes, so large, almost purple, and so intelligent, sensitive, and remorseful right now, that both her fear, and grim resolve to endure it, broke. She felt her own eyes liquefy with unshed tears.

"I know," she whispered back. "It's just…your teeth…so very large…and your species so new to me." No longer smiling, she felt her eyes spill over.

"Littler Librrtee-huh," he said in a low, tender growl, "I'll go slow and careful, but must finish rites. Is assent with you?"

She nodded. Slowly, with mouth closed, and keeping their eyes locked, he swayed her cradled in his arms, smelling her ears, then her neck, then between her breasts, looking up at her. His six fingers unlocked, and he separated her ass cheeks, holding each globe in one paw so that her labia parted a bit. He lifted her up again as his nose slowly pressed between breasts, grazing past the purple velvet stuff encasing her belly, and then down to where her net-weave skirt allowed his snout fur to softly bristle through to the tops of her thighs and pubic hair as he breathed in her scent.

A strange lassitude filled her. Even as his long large furred fingers spread more widely and parted her thighs further, she helped open herself to him by raising her knees a little and bracing her hands on his velvet shoulders. He was blowing his warm breath on her labia, then huffing in slowly. He bounced her minutely in his hands, letting one side of her ass weigh down first, then the other. Her labial lips kissed against each other. His fingers pressed close by, fur and bones and flesh felt, their pressure a slight remove from her labia itself. Though he didn't directly touch her there, she felt his presence in her pussy. She was becoming wet and sensitive. She knew he could smell it.

"Grrr," he rumbled quietly. "You. Better now. Smell clean mating. Bg'rpbleek chooses well."

He pushed her ass forward as he lowered her so that her thighs parted further and her pussy was split open on his chest, feeling the million tiny prickles of his fur. His hands rhythmically squeezed her ass against him as he slowly, slowly slid her down him, her wetness trailing its scent on him, slicking his fur flat in a slowly painted stripe.

She inhaled his own wild animal smell sharply, gave a slight gasp. Had Dunn and the other Bear heard? Her cheeks pressed his forehead as he swayed his face back and forth under her jaw, still looking up at her with huge dark eyes. She felt heat rise to her cheeks as he lowered her more slowly till he paused, eye level again. Parting his mouth just enough to dart out his purple-black, gleaming tongue, he licked her lips with it, mashing her pelvis hard against his belly, and stuck the enormous, thick muscle of his tongue between her teeth as his forefingers and thumbs curled closer to touch her labia directly. They sculpted her lips and clitoris as his tongue washed the roof and walls of her mouth.

She was panting in time with him, and started to nurse on his tongue. The furred fingers that still held her off the ground were an exquisitely foreign sensation. Her pussy poured out its honey, juicing down the fur of his bulbous-ended fingers. A thumb and forefinger suddenly pulled a fold of flesh over her clitoral nub and rolled her swelling clit beneath it, so that one second she felt his fingers gloved with her own skin, and the next felt his furred thumb directly, prickling her moist pearl and inner lips.

He pulled his tongue from the suction of her mouth and pressed hairless thin lips to hers. She dug her hands into his shoulders and pulled the fur she found there. His eyes smiled.

She found herself looking up at him now as he pulled her down past his soft belly hairs and slowly removed his fingers to make way for a fist-sized leather-skinned knob that rubbed at her entrance. Her nether lips sucked at its egg-shaped contours, and slid along down the outer swell of something ridged that felt thick as her husband's wrist. It seemed to her that it widened gradually after each ridge, as if the organ was more cone-shaped than man's.

It felt like this corduroy effect went on for two feet, but she hoped this was only because Fangor was drawing her so slowly along down its length. She shuddered to imagine it full inside her. She heard Fangor's mate growl.

Her legs by now were wrapped fully around him, her cunt as open on him as she could make it. Her spider-web skirt was up to her waist as he drew her down over a huge furred swelling containing at least four balls beneath that exotic cock. She could feel herself blushing for excitement and embarrassment at being witnessed by their mates in this blatant exercise, but her nightside coloring kept its secret.

Fangor planted her feet on floor, squeezing her ass firmly one more time, and flicking his thumbs over her labial petals and clit, then in the most leisurely manner imaginable, dragging one hand down around her ass and in front to her bush of hair, pressing into it firmly, as his other hand slid a long forefinger up into her cunt and out again in farewell. He drew himself up and a few inches away from her. Her skirt fell down slowly as a curtain in soft breeze.

They stood there, both their nostrils flaring. She looked over at Dunn. He looked more horrified than she, but was oblivious to her dilemma. Evidently, he had been undergoing his own drama with Bigger.

His body was arched away from the giant female, but his groin was pointed as if magnetized toward her snout where she hunched over him. It was clearly fully hard through the leathern tights, and she could see its dark purpling head inched above the waistband, which had been pulled down to reveal it.

Bigger blew hard between her teeth and through her nose at Dunn's straining cock; then her large blue-purple tongue, which outsized his cock (itself not an inconsiderable size for a human's), curled out and lapped it, and wrapped it like a blue corn tortilla, currently popular on the Station.

Dunn felt Liberty's glance. His eyes cornered towards her.

"Liberty?" His voice squeaked. "Help!"

Bigger glanced over at her and grinned. She uncoupled her tongue from Dunn with a slurp.

"GOOD MATE YOU HAVE!" she thundered approvingly.

Liberty gaped back, speechless. These Bears were crazed with sex, infecting her and Dunn. Escape, escape!

Bigger picked Dunn up one-handed by the waist, thumbed down the rest of his waistband to free his cock completely, and ground it into her shaggy breastless chest.

He cried wildly once more: "Liberty! HELP!"

A serbot hovered with brandy bulbs and asked, "More brandy? Or are you in distress? Is this an emergency?"

Even from his present position, he and Liberty exchanged considering glances. Dunn began to look less panicked; if they needed it, help was immediately available. He looked a question at her. She was thinking the same thing, she knew: a public clamor? Proving they were incompetent at handling off-Station, other-world guests of alien species? Humiliating; very likely reducing their hard-won status.

They both shook their heads "no". She loved Dunn for his similar outlook. Even more so at a time like this.

"Ignore all cries for help," she instructed the serbot. She could always rescind this instruction. If the Bears started eating them. Bigger and Fangor watched this exchange, began bellowing in Krynner at each other. Liberty covered her ears in pain.

Fangor yelped once at his mate and both quieted a bit.

"SUCH HONOR! We begin...dance....party."

"And both us receptive now!" Bigger crowed over to her. Her free paw ripped Dunn's tights to shreds and flung them down.

Liberty was immediately distracted as Fangor leaned over to her breasts, curling back his lips to expose only the points of his teeth, and as his jaw whiskered her left breast like thick velvet, he

20

caught the edge of her blouse with those teeth and peeled it down till the one breast swam out. He brushed her nipple softly again and again with his facial fur, nuzzling it to hardness, opened his teeth again and slowly, inexorably, clenched his teeth tight on its swollen tit-bit. He worried it gently, pulled it long as it would stretch, then twisted it first left, then right, between gleaming fangs. Only her nipple separated those upper and lower fangs. He bit down, drawing no blood.

What big teeth he had! But *they* were no longer what frightened her. He had considerable control over them, as he proved by scraping her nipple between them till he'd tormented a little moan from her.

On her own feet, in their unaccustomed high heels, she lost her balance and toppled suddenly away, her nipple breaking contact with his teeth. He grabbed her one-handed between the legs, hard, righting her, then lifted her up off the floor. Gravity pressed her full weight against his palm, centered in her ever-wetter pussy. She *was* that center of herself, in that puddle of wet flesh against hot, fur-edged palm.

He suddenly pushed up with all his might; she was airborne for a moment, then his other palm caught her in the same way. She smacked down with a wet, slurping splash of sound that they both heard. He was juggling her! She was too transported to laugh. She and Dunn had never explored this as a possibility in the Station's low gravity; they were too closely matched in size, but the Bear was big enough to toss and catch her. He threw her up in to the air and caught her once more, his left palm wet with her oils.

Then he took her by the waist with his other arm, squeezing the breath from her, and brought his free hand up to his snout, inhaling.

"YOU READY," he intoned. His eyes seized hers. With both hands, he held her lightly, parallel to the floor, and tore off her skirt with his teeth. She heard delicate fabric rip. Goodbye antique! She was past caring.

Holding her like a sandwich toward his mouth, he spanked one leg over his shoulder, then the other, till her sweet morsel faced his snout. The thick purple tongue emerged, as huge as her hand. Muscular, wet, slightly rasping, it pulled her mount up and enveloped her clitoris. His tongue dragged the entire pad of her vulva up towards her belly. She rocked into that unyielding muscle. Cunt aflame, she moved her legs against his velvet neck and shoulders, then pressed her heels hard into his back. It didn't seem to hurt him. The skin-tight tops of her boots rolled down over her knees.

Slowly she was lowered to the floor, as he bent over her, still lapping at her. She felt his tongue curl into a tube and push past her inner lips, entering her swollen flesh deeply, its bumpy texture exquisite. It was larger than Dunn's penis, and just as hard.

Her heart was hammering, rhythm of desire and panic at once. (If his tongue was this big, how much larger would that penis get? She would never let that happen! She *wasn't* his species!) His rough-grained tongue entered her again, withdrew, entered her, withdrew. Entered her.

She pushed her hands at his chest. His snout came away, glistening threads of her own desire hanging from those thin ursine lips.

"So soon want more of me?" he asked happily. He leaned his body over her prone figure. His penis grazed her knees. Its ridged length throbbed against her thighs as it came further up her body. His belly fleece brushed her bare skin in thrilling sensation.

She reached up her arms and grabbed his ears. That got his attention.

"NO! Please! You could kill me!"

His laugh a low rumble: "Not possible, Librr-tee-huh. You will know. Safe."

Only his lower belly met her body now as he arched his long torso in a "C", to keep his head at her head's level, yet bring his groin area close to hers. Her thighs felt everywhere soft soft down, but for that hard-skinned pole pressing closer and closer.

She *knew* he would be too large for her, but her body denied her brain's logic: her thighs loosened at their joints, and turned out with more slack, allowing him unguarded entrance. She *wanted* to believe him. She wanted it possible. Surely he'd just enter halfway, then stop, if she yelled. Her mind drifted.

The top of his cock's spherical head lolled at her vagina's entrance. It was as large as the brandy bulb. She moaned.

He pushed the head in past the first ring of muscle. She wondered how she had managed to stretch that wide, but Macrocosm! it felt wonderful.

"How large you are!"

"As large as you want, my Librr-tee-huh."

He played with her for a long while, that sphere moving out, moving in, the same amount repeatedly. Each time he withdrew, he pointed it up at the last second, to massage her clit with the full round surface of it, spreading a thick jammy balm that oozed from it, and pressing her clit a little flatter against her pubic bone every time. Her womb fluttered in time to their dance.

Then its entrance into her changed. The round bulb pushed higher into her, at a slant now, and rode hardest into the wall beneath her belly. Hard rings of ridged flesh slowly widened her inner lips and drove in, stretching her impossibly wider and wider with every accordion-rib of its length. She felt her cunt stretch beyond a size she had ever imagined accommodating.

Frightened, with her pussy feeling milky and transparent and still hunting his cock's length and finding no end, she breathed her fear to him.

"Enough…enough…how much of you is in?"

Fangor gazed at her, oval pupils so wise and black, very little purple-brown iris could be seen. His eyes looked shiny, alien, yet familiar in their insanity of lust. First he growled in Kynner, a low vibration she felt through her skin, chest to breasts, and penetrating cock to cunt; then switched to Galactic.

"I remain most of me outside," he panted. "We go slow. Not worry. Feeled good?" He withdrew a few inches, then penetrated her the same small amount again.

"Hunnnghh!" she replied.

The pressure she felt as he stretched her yet wider by 2 more rings of cock made her heart jump into her throat. She decided right then to forego the antique pleasures of actual childbirth she had previously considered.

"No more! Please! No! More!"

"I have surpassed maximum pleasure width?" He saw by the rictus of her face that he probably had. "One ring less? Two rings?"

As he asked, he did something she could scarcely follow or credit. The circumference of her invader *shrank* to the width of the preceding inch he had sunk in her, without withdrawing any of his length that was already within her. Yet his cock did not deflate; it remained equally hard.

"All that size good? Best?" he asked with growled concern.

"How…did…you *do* that?" she gasped.

"Grstl'k's bred to fit for sized needed" he told her. "I probe you now."

He entered her with more of his cock, ring by ring, but no longer larger with each inch. Her clit felt like it was skating along a bumpy road. Amazed, she let herself go into her own pleasure at its touch. His cock's corduroy texture made her feel as if she was being entered anew with every new ridge, her own rings of inner muscle squeezing down in spasms to hug each thickness anew. He sped up the rate with which he entered her, and now her clit was speeding down a rollercoaster of juddering rails.

The spherical head jammed hard into her cervix, then pushed at it, filling her as much as she could take.

"Length enough?" His low mutter.

"Yes!"

"Now we begin."

He pulled out a little faster than he had entered her, and eyeballed her measurements that stopped at the top third of his cock.

"Size is good?"

She nodded, looking at his big Bear cock. It was shrinking before her very eyes to the amount he'd just sunk into her. She stroked it in amazement, now feeling his furred balls (all four of them!) much closer to the bulbous head. He preened and clasped her hand within his to wrap around his still rock-hard but smaller, (relatively) manageable-sized cock.

"We dance now," he commanded. "New way for you, new way for me. Or you say…frek? I frek you, you frek me. Frek starts now."

For a quick second, she glanced over at Dunn and Bigger. Dunn was lapping at the SheBear's furred chest, which was shining with a milky liquid. Her husband was groaning, sunk into her. Bigger held his head on her flat breast and suckled him, stroking his ass with her other hand. Like mammals, they must lactate, she guessed.

Distracting her from that other scene, Fangor entered her again, as huge as he'd felt in the beginning, but this time she was fearless. He was still so big she ached, but her thighs shuddered and she flailed her legs, sinking bootheels into his flanks as he sank himself into her again and again. She came fully at his sixth stroke, but he never wavered.

"I come to know you." Then he lost his Galactic and just growled loudly. She didn't shrink at his bellowing, but joined in.

Her captor's rhythm made her come and come and come. *He* was the one who varied their positions, sometimes jumping up as she clung on, the extra g-force thrusting into her in a most satisfactory way, sometimes bouncing her so high off him in the low-grav that she seemed to hover before she crashed down to spear herself again on his cock. Always, *he* chose the change of pose, *he* picked her up like she was weightless, *he* set the pace of her orgasms. When she struggled to gain a little control, or tried to make him come, he barked a laugh and juggled her by her pussy again. She lost count of time.

Finally, he took her neck between those long curved teeth, pressing down his fangs to gently pinch her carotid artery, and shook her with his head. Arching her throat back in those great jaws, she surrendered fully, prepared to either die or orgasm beneath him again. Weakly, she felt herself lose consciousness as the pressure of his bite cut off the blood to her head. He rammed his alien organ into her ferociously, impaling her; then, opening his jaws with a deafening roar, he shot his animal joy into her on this last stroke. Her head cleared, oxygen rushing back to her brain, and she came yet again, in a series of spasms, orgasms beyond count.

Alien jelly filled her battered pussy. Pounds of it. So, he had not eaten her.

The Bears had left, gone home. Liberty and Dunn stared in exhaustion at each other.

Liberty sat with her legs open slackly, the tendons sprung. Her cunt gaped at him, swollen and still slick and shining at him with Fangor's juices, mixed with his own.

Dunn's rectum was full of these same Fangor juices. He wondered that he had never before been aware of exquisite…sensation… in that area in all his entire previous existence.

Two days of sexual frenzy with two crazed Bears. And they were damned if they could ever admit it to another soul on the Station. Their research was unpublishable.

When both recovered, they would make love slowly and tenderly, and he would marvel at her human beauty, her two dark breasts (two only!), her pale eyes, her almost hairless skin. Such a relief to become erect for human beauty. How had that repulsive SheBear ever even gotten him hard? he wondered: drugs slipped into their brandy? hormones? some universal pheromone in the liquids her four nipples had expressed, and which she had forced him to lap, till frenzied, he'd managed to fuck her?

He also recalled both Bears forcing Liberty and him to … perform…before them. He had even used her pet-name in their hearing.

Large, furry, fanged people, *ha!* Large furry fanged oversexed… *hominids*. Bears. Thank the Cosmos they'd never have to set eyes on them again.

~~-o0O0o-~~

It took Liberty two months to realize just what the Bears had done to her. Somehow, they'd managed to counteract the antifertility med's she inhaled once a month. She knew in her bones they were to blame, 'though she went through the motions of requesting a diagnostic of the mist sequence of their serbot-programmed shower.

Neither she nor Dunn could recall any drug being given them during the Bears' visit, but in the throngs of their…heat…would either of them have noticed a skinsolv?

Liberty worried her lower lip – not at the problem; the Bears were naïve to think humans without recourse to such antique dilemmas – but the thought blistered her: what *else* had they done to her, to Dunn? *Why* would they wish to choose for a human couple to have offspring at this time?

Later that same day, the stellagram arrived.

"Mutual congratulations to both us, from us!" it blurted. "My womb swells in sympath. Have with great pride of entire Grstl'k clan informed our home planet Chancellor of all Krynnr. Also your Ambassador here. Our offspring will bless this the first intergalactic simultaneous conceptions of your species and ours! How envies His Worship Garl Krbgrs of Vledj, who sends his regards. Let's meet up when childrings reach 10 standard Galactics. Healthy bear us!" A formal sign-off ended it.

Garl Krbgrs sent them rare orchids from his home planet. The attached card read merely: "In thanks for your hospitality – Carl Crabgrass."

The lovely black and blue blooms unfortunately soon developed a putrid scent, akin to the worst Planetsider cheeses that had long been banned on Spaceships. It took weeks to scrub the smell from their living pod.

--o0O0o--

Forced to have this child for reasons of intergalactic diplomacy, Liberty had borne it for the full nine months *in utero*; Medical had planned to transplant it to the safer, sterile environment of standard Station fetal incubation, but all her tests had countermanded this most routine procedure.

It was then they had received the second shock. The Bears had done more than merely override her contraceptives. They had altered her womb's very chemistry, and, the Stalwarts presumed grimly, their infant's as well. The tests all came back atypical – undecipherable.

By the time Fraternity was born (and Liberty had *had* to endure all the antique charms of animal birth she'd once been tempted by, lest other options queer the unknown chemistries at work in her body), they had learned more of Bear society, biology, science. So Fraternity's all-over fur was not the shock it might once have been.

The Bears lived for DNA-grafting, it seemed. Species-wide hobby. Their science had been coöpted into their very bodies; basically each Bear was a walking chem-lab. They could analyze anything by taste; synthesize by ingestion; alter by a Bear sort of yoga.

Their Bear-Human orgy had combined three DNA strands into two new species: their own poor dear deformed Fraternity, and the monster the Bears called Kritter.

The Stalwarts sacrificed the lawn, the flowers, the off-Station guests. They retired to a more private sphere, in an outer, quieter ring of the Station, just a simple plant geneticist and gyrotational math mech and their school-going daughter. (The whole Station deemed them very brave, and said so continually.) Though as political celebrities, they perforce gave an interview once every standard solar, grinning for the vizzies trained on them by intergalactic documusement teams. Like bears in a zoo.

Only Fraternity enjoyed these. Each year she became even more popular amongst the ShipChildren, who relished messaging their peers on other Stations – or even Planetsiders – that the famous Fraternity was their close personal friend. (A youth trend for hairiness caught on, making its way up the generations; previously-depilated adults suddenly clamored for body hair.)

They themselves watched vizzies of the Bears and their growing son Kritter, colored like a blond Polar Bear: black-skinned, turquoise-eyed, fur yellower than it was white.

"Liberty's color so entertained us," explained Bigger to a Vledjan interviewer. "Of course, with Kritter, we could only mimic with Dunn's recessives – Kritter has none of her DNA – but we did not want her to feel left out of the creation we all shared."

It was a high compliment, Liberty realized glumly, and they had made sure that the DNA she did contribute to her daughter's continued the phenotype that so entertained them: Fraternity shared the Liberty tri-colors.

The Vledjan news-muse then next asked Bigger for "an intimate portrait" of this creation they had all shared, and as Bigger obliged with vivid details ("We learned she prefers using name GildenPelt during sex only, improves arousal time"), and then an uncut vizzie she had evidently shot with an implant eye-cam, Liberty clapped it off.

She noted with disgust that she'd become wet, aroused by the memories. Her biggest fear was coming truer every year: she was learning too much about Bears. She wished that she, Dunn and Fraternity could become immune to them.

--o0O0o--

But of course having met several times as children, then as teenagers, the Bears' giant little son and their own tall furred daughter fell in love; became engaged; married.

The ceremony was attended by fashionably-hirsute diplomats from many worlds, horrible numbers of Bears, and of course, all four of the lucky parents. Everyone dressed formally, she herself in six turquoise art-silk panels that fell to the floor from her shoulders and arms, revealing ribbons of her skin in dark contrast whenever she moved. Dunn in similar panels of black, with turquoise padded codpiece and pectoral-plates. The bride and groom wore elaborate headpieces and nothing else.

She shuddered at the feel of Fangor's gaze on her once again. Memories coursed through her body. She arched her back at the chemistry.

"Librr-tee-huh, dear lady," Fangor approached her like a dancer. "We meet again, in the flesh! The vizzies have not done you justice – the years have been kind."

Giant shoulders stooped, and he kissed the air beside each cheek in a snuffle, barely brushing her with his beard. She blushed, gazing into purple eyes again.

"And didn't we make a splendid daughter?" he asked intently. She suddenly guessed that he had not only mastered Galactic in the intervening years; he must have read up on their culture, understood the violation they had committed, despite the pleasure they'd given them. Given her.

"We did indeed," she assured him. "Fraternity is a wonderful girl – med-degree'd at eleven! – any pair of fathers would be proud." With her Bear-bestown chem-lab nose, she had indeed sailed through medschool.

Fangor grinned shyly. "And Kritter – your husband's genes such a magnificent gift! They will blend again with yours in the next generation: Kritter and Fraternity's offspring."

He raised a champagne flute to hers. They chimed glasses gently. "A toast to Fraternity and Kritter's children: a new species! They will call him Equality." And so she learned of her daughter's pregnancy.

She politely slogged down the fine wine: tasteless stuff now.

"You are courteous indeed to not hate us for our inadvertent trespass," Fangor whispered softly in her ear. "We have both – our cultures – learned so much in this time. To make love to other species first, just for pleasure – and to ask before making pregnant. Would you like this, GildenPelt?" Dunn's private name for her, on Fangor's tongue, shocked her. He had not called her by it previously, although the vizzied interview years ago made it clear they'd heard Dunn say it, during the demonstration of human intercourse they'd given the Bears. Its use by Dunn was always prelude to sex. Her pussy reacted. She was moist. I could want this Bear all over again, she marvelled. What's wrong with my brain? Or pussy?

"There is a room here…" He darted his eyes toward the end of the large hall.

She was thankfully interrupted from having to answer as Kritter, resplendent in bejeweled green turban, leapt over to them. A young god of Krnnyrdom, she realized. His human qualities made him sexier than either father. Fraternity had lucked out over many a Bearmaiden, Liberty realized for the first time.

"Bridesmother," he bowed, then straightened to grin at her with Fangor's same carnal grin. He was, at 2 meters tall, Fraternity's exact height. Kritter gazed down at her feet, then ever-so-slowly swept his eyes up, over every inch of her. "You will visit us, I hope?" he asked winsomely. She realized there was no taboo in offering himself; she wasn't his parent. She could see it now, the full meaning of Bears' welcome to houseguest. One she and Dunn had once inadvertently made.

"Of course," she smiled back, lying. "And you'll stay with us? At the Station, I mean? We have wonderful guest quarters."

Kritter's face fell. She guessed she felt complimented at his disappointment.

She might not see her daughter again for years. She'd lost her to the Krnnyr genetic inheritance. She could never say what Kritter and Fangor said now to her, in unison:

"Our home is your home!"

Smiling noncommittal thanks, Liberty caught Fangor's eye, then glanced meaningfully at the room he'd indicated. Unhurriedly, she swayed over to the royal-green velvet curtains that puddled either side of a discreet door. The turquoise panels of her outfit created a little breeze and a little friction as she sashayed, perking her dark nipples to hard candies. She bent over as if retrieving something she'd dropped, the blue-green silk waterfalling in the middle over either side of both legs, revealing her ass to him, along with a glimpse of her gildenpelt, a mere hint of glistening lips. She could smell him following her in.

Colette Torrez *is the nom de plume of a Lady who does not wish her reputation to be sullied by the occasionally salacious nature of her imagination, which she has fully indulged in this tale. t. She grew up travelling: California, Ireland, Indiana, New York. It is her firm belief that the schools she attended in Ireland, which ranged from the proverbial two-room schoolhouse – where her Uncle and great-grandparents taught – to the strictest of convent schools, have most influenced her depraved tastes in literature. An ordained minister as well as an artist, Ms. Torrez now resides in Jamaica Plain, Massachusetts where she raises a sloth of black bears with which she supplies a very-specialized film industry.*

CITY WITHOUT
A RIVER
by Joe Ambrose

Tangier is a city without a river. A river of sorts makes its way into the sea down the east end of town near the new train station but that is more of a wadi or a sewer than a river as we understand it in the colder north.

When we had finisher our exertions she retired to the bathroom and showered. I went to the kitchen and released the kitten cat from her frosty prison.

She was not quite frozen but she sure was frosty and had a terrified confused aspect to her demeanour. Why had she not meowed in demand of her freedom from the pitch-black freezer? Why had she confined herself to scratching the ice with such a frenzy that the icy walls of the freezer were pink with her blood?

By way of some sort of a consolation prize I I gave her fresh milk and raw tuna steak – tuna I'd intended using in the construction of a tuna salad later that evening for myself and Badar. Terrified or traumatised, this didn't stop the cat from eating her fill.

The receptionist from the Minzah Hotel emerged from the bathroom refreshed and fully dressed. Oh, she was a dog to go! She glanced distastefully at the cat. "Ah, you has cat?" she asked spitefully like some jealous lover. "Filthy thing the cat."

And I said, smiling beatifically, "Yes, filthy thing the pussy. It is not mine; it just came in from the street."

"You let filthy street cat into your home? Huh!"

Soon she was on the street outside hailing a Petit Taxi which would take her to the Minzah where she was due on duty mid-afternoon.

Soon the cat was back on the street with her mother who'd missed her and searched frantically for her while she was confined to my freezer. Both of them basked calmly in the golden autumnal sun – though my erstwhile prisoner looked cautiously over her shoulder at me from time to time.

That was six years ago and now I am far away and I am living in a city with a river running right down its middle.

Oh I miss my pussy now growing old and cold in that far away hot city without a river.

Joe Ambrose works as a writer, filmmaker, and arts agitator. A member of Islamic Diggers, described as "rai-hop terrorists" by The Wire, he co-produced the CD which features tracks by Paul Bowles, Bill Laswell, The Master Musicians of Joujouka, Marianne Faithfull, Chuck Prophet, John Cale, Scanner, and William Burroughs.

HOME IS THE SAILOR
by William Miekle

I smoked too many cigarettes, sipped too much Highland Park and let Bessie Smith tell me just how bad men were. For once thin afternoon sun shone on Glasgow; the last traces of winter just a distant memory. Old Joe started up "Just One Cornetto" in the shop downstairs. I didn't have a case, and I didn't care.

It was Easter weekend, and all was right with the world.

I should have known it was too good to last.

I heard him coming up the stairs. Sherlock Holmes could have told you his height, weight, shoe-size and nationality from the noise he made. All I knew was that he was either ill or very old; he'd taken the stairs like he was climbing a mountain with a Sherpa on his back.

He rapped on the outside door.

Shave and a haircut, two bits.

"Come in. Adams Massage Services is open for business."

At first I thought it was someone wandering in off the street. He was unkempt, unshaven, eyes red and bleary. He wore an old brown wool suit over a long, out of shape cardigan and his hair stood out from his scalp in strange clumps. I've rarely seen a man more in need of a drink.

Or a meal.

He was so thin as to be almost skeletal, the skin on his face stretched tight across his cheeks. I was worried that if I made him smile his face might split open like an over-ripe fruit.

"Are you Adams?" he said as he came in. He turned out to be younger than I'd first taken him for, somewhere in his fifties at a guess, but his mileage was much higher. "Jim at the Twa Dugs said you might be able to help me."

I waved him in.

"It's about time Jim started calling in some of the favors I owe him. Sit down Mr...?"

"Duncan. Ian Duncan."

He sat, perched at the front of the chair, as if afraid to relax. His eyes flickered around the room, never staying long on anything, never looking straight at me.

"Smoke?" I asked, offering him the packet.

He shook his head.

"It might kill me," he said.

I lit up anyway... a smell wafted from the man, a thick oily tang so strong that even the pungent Camels didn't help much.

Time for business.

"So what can I do for you, Mr. Duncan?"

"I'm going to die sometime this weekend. I need you to stop them."

I stared back at him.

"Sounds like a job for the Polis to me," I said.

He laughed, making it sound like a sob. He took a bundle of fifty pound notes from his pocket and slapped them on the table. I tried not to salivate.

"No. This is no job for the terminally narrow-minded," he said. "I need somebody with a certain kind of experience. *Your* kind of experience."

Somebody put a cold brick in my stomach, and I had a sudden urge to stick my fingers in my ears. I got the whisky out of the drawer. I offered him one. He shook his head, but his eyes didn't stray from the bottle. I poured his measure into a glass alongside my own and sent them chasing after each other before speaking.

"And exactly what kind of experience do I need to help you?"

A good storyteller practices his tale. At first, when he tells the story, he sounds like your dad ruining his favorite dinner table joke for the hundredth time.

Oh wait... did I tell you the horse had a pig with him?

But gradually he begins to understand the rhythm of the story, and how it depends on knowing all the little details, even the ones that no one ever sees or hears. He knows what color of trousers he was wearing the day the story took place, he knows that the police dog had a bad leg, he knows that the toilet block smelled of piss and shit. He has the sense of place so firmly in his mind that even he almost believes he's been there. Once he's done all that, he tells the killer story, complete with unexpected punch line.

Then there's the Ian Duncan method... scatter information about like confetti and hope that somebody can put enough of it together to figure out what had happened to who.

I raised an eyebrow, and that was enough to at least get him started.

"It was four years ago we bought the hotel in Largs," he started.

"Well there's your first mistake," I replied, but he didn't acknowledge me. Now that he'd started the story, he meant to finish it. The tale he told would have been outlandish to anyone else's ears, but like he'd said, I knew better, from bitter experience.

I let him finish – sick customers, ancient curse and all, before asking the important question.

"And how do you think I can help?"

Just telling me the story had taken it out of him. I forced a glass of whisky on him – it was either that or watch him die in the chair. He almost choked on it, but managed to keep it all down before replying.

"Come down for the weekend. There's a room I need you to see. Maybe you'll be able to make sense of it where I can't."

I *wanted* to say no, but he'd put his money on the table, and that got him my attention. Besides, his story had me intrigued, and I hadn't been *doon the watter* to Largs since I was a lad.

What better time than a holiday weekend?

--oOOo--

Largs is where old people go to die – a Victorian seaside resort that is itself dying slowly of neglect. The Vikings tried to sack it eight hundred years ago. Maybe it would have been better all round if they'd succeeded.

I'd spent many long weekend trips here as a lad. My parents couldn't afford to go any further afield, and to a young boy one beach was as good as another, even if the weather was rarely good enough to take advantage on the long patch of golden sand to the south of the town. As I got off the train I could already see that the place hadn't changed much. It was raining, that steady drizzle peculiar to the west of Scotland, the kind that you just *know* is going to last all week.

Luckily I didn't have to go far. Duncan had given me instructions before leaving me in the office, but I could have found it with my eyes shut as it was on the sea front, two hotels down from the Barrfields theatre and next to the putting green where my dad used to swear for Scotland.

The Seaview Hotel lived on past glories from the days when the middle class of Glasgow filled it every weekend of the summer. Back in the twenties it had been the height of fashion, but now it exuded the faint whiff of decay. It was a rambling, Edwardian building, with thirty rooms and nearly as many corridors. The décor was all mock-Scottish; dark furniture, stuffed stag heads and heavy on the tartan for wallpaper and carpets; a hideous red and yellow that clashed with everything else in the hotel.

Duncan met me in the hallway and led me through to the dining room. There were six patrons sitting at a table by the bay window, and not one of them looked like they were going to last out the day, being as thin and wasted as Duncan.

"What's going on here?" I asked.

Duncan led me to the far side of the room.

"I told you," he said. "The curse..."

I waved him away and lit up a smoke. It improved the smell, but not by much.

"Aye. The curse," I said. "Some time in the Twenties you said?"

He kept his voice low.

"Jim McLeod was an old Navy man. He retired to Largs with his wife and had this place built. It was to be their dream home, but she died before it could be finished. After that McLeod became a collector," he said. "And he wasn't fussy about where he bought his pieces. Many of them were stolen to order from other collectors or museums. The story goes that someone took umbrage and laid a curse on the whole hotel."

I nodded.

"But here's what I don't get. Why now?"

Duncan didn't reply, but I saw a look in his eyes I recognised. He was hiding something. And he was afraid to the point of abject terror. I took pity on him.

"Let's cut to the chase. Show me this room you told me about, and we'll see if we can get to the bottom of this."

--o0O0o--

The room at the highest point of the hotel was packed wall to wall with antiques. Even to my unpractised eye I knew that there was a small fortune just lying there in the accumulated dust. From the look of things McLeod's passion had been African tribal masks, and a variety of them leered down from the walls interspersed with weapons and beaded necklaces. But the thing that Duncan had brought me here to see was spread out under a pane of glass in a long display case.

At first glance it looked like a crude map, tracing a journey across Africa, ending at the mouth of the Zambezi river.

"McLeod thought it belonged to David Livingstone," Duncan said. "But I can't see it myself. Livingstone was a devout man of God. He wouldn't have anything to do with this depravity."

I saw what he meant as I leaned for a closer look. What I had taken for paper was in fact skin, so thin as to be almost translucent. I didn't have to ask the question.

A map made on human skin, drawn in blood.

I had a good look at it, but it seemed I had already got as much information as I was going to get. Duncan was looking at me expectantly.

"Well, what do you think?" he asked.

I was still unsure exactly what he wanted from me. Sure, the curse *seemed* to be working... residents in the hotel were certainly wasting away beyond even what you'd expect in a pensioner's graveyard like Largs.

But how could I find out why?

I only knew one man who might help, and I was loath to involve him. I'd damaged my good friend Doug enough in too many cases. He was at his happiest right where he now spent most of his time, deep in the stacks of the Hunterian Museum storerooms.

I sent him a couple of pictures by email from my cell-phone, knowing even as I hit Send that it might be some time before he got back to his desk to receive them. In the meantime, I needed to maintain the illusion that I knew what I was doing.

"Let's have a chat with your guests," I said to Duncan.

He looked shocked at the suggestion.

"That might not be such a good idea," he said, but he allowed me to lead the way back downstairs.

~~-o0O0o-~~

My plan to interview the guests came to nothing, mainly because two of them were dead face down in their soup, and the other four were too far-gone to notice.

Duncan showed little concern, and only became agitated on my mention of calling the Police.

"There's no need for that, Mr. Adams," he said. Once he'd written me a cheque for an extra five grand I came to agree with him. I helped him drag the bodies out of the dining room. It took little effort – the old folks weighed no more than a small child at most.

Duncan had me take them out the back of the hotel and left me alone for a minute – long enough for me to wonder if the five grand was enough.

To either side the adjoining hotels had bowling-green flat lawns, lush and verdant. The Seaview on the other hand looked like someone had ploughed the lawn over, leaving lumps and bumps across the whole surface. It was only when Duncan came back with two shovels that I realised why.

Duncan held out a shovel but I ignored him.

"Just how long have you been burying guests out here?"

He wouldn't meet my gaze, and mumbled, but I caught the vital word.

Years.

"Please," he said, holding the shovel out to me, his eyes pleading. "No one need ever know."

But I will.

I left him to it and went in search of a drink.

--o0O0o--

One advantage to an almost empty hotel is that the bar is quiet, and a man can smoke with impunity. I helped myself to a large scotch and lit up a Camel. By the time I got on to the second scotch I was starting to feel more myself, and the large cheque in my pocket had me feeling much more sanguine about the situation. I thought matters had improved when my phone beeped and I got a text message from Doug.

No real idea beyond burning it, it said,

Burning it. There's a thought.

I took a third Scotch upstairs with me. I checked out the window when I got to the top room. Duncan was still out on the lawn, knee-deep in a growing hole. I was about to burn his property, but then again, he'd brought me here to stop the curse, and that's what I intended to do.

I had to take a spear from the wall to prise the glass case open, having to slice and chip at glue that had gone rock hard. I'd finished the third whisky by the time I was done, but finally I was able to lift the lid.

The thing felt slimy to the touch, almost warm. It got warmer still as I flicked the Zippo and applied the flame to a corner. It took fast – so fast that it went up with a *whoosh* and I had to drop it to avoid getting singed. I stood back as it blazed itself down to a charred black mass on a now equally charred carpet.

I was feeling pleased with myself... right up until the screams rose up from out in the back garden. As I moved to the window my

40

phone rang. I answered it on the way, just in time to read the full transcript of Doug's text that had been split into two messages.

"No real idea beyond burning it... would not be recommended."

Bugger.

Things got even worse when I looked down from the window.

Duncan had backed away, holding a shovel like an axe, smacking it again and again on the head of one of the recently deceased.

Or maybe not so deceased.

The withered thing pushed herself upright, shakily at first, then more sure of herself as she started to stagger forwards. There was more life in her now than there had been before she *died*.

Duncan hit her again, screaming in fury.

"Die you old bitch, die," he shouted. The old woman tripped, but didn't fall. She opened her mouth and clacked her teeth together. The effect was spoiled when the false top set slipped out and fell wetly to the grass, but she didn't slow. Duncan screamed one last time then fled for the back door of the hotel.

I should have gone to his aid, but I was dumbstruck by the view below me.

The whole lawn seethed and roiled, as if a great beast struggled to break through the blanket of grass. But this was no single beast. The first indication was a pale arm bursting with some force through the sod, grasping for a hold. More arms pushed through; some pale, some grey, some green and moist with decay, but all grasping.

I remembered Duncan's answer when asked how long he'd been burying bodies.

Years.

Even as they dragged their re-born bodies up out of the lawn, screams rose up through the hotel from below. I grabbed the spear I'd used to open the display case and made for the stairs.

~-o0O0o-~

Duncan was once more the source of the screaming. I found him in the rear scullery, fighting to hold the back door closed against a press of bodies. They were packed tightly around the door, a crowd of what looked like over twenty, coming forward slowly. At first all that could be seen were silhouettes, dark shadows against the strong daylight beyond. But when they approached the glass door, it became all too clear what they were.

They had once been pensioners, but they'd been too long in Largs... far too long. Some of them were in better condition than others were, but all shared one common, open-mouthed expression, teeth and gums working in expectation of food.

The outside door of the bar crashed open and the press of bodies fought in a scrum trying to reach us.

"Bastards!" Duncan shouted, as the first of them pushed into the scullery itself.

It had once been a woman, dressed in an expensive tweed two piece suit and Gucci shoes. Now she missed one of her heels. She lurched from side to side like a drunken sailor.

I stepped forward and slammed the spear into her chest.

She staggered backwards, but only for a second. By the time she came forward again three more of her kind had pushed through into the scullery.

I felt something tug at my arm. It was Duncan.

"Mr. Adams," the hotel owner said. "I really think we should be going."

I shoved the old man ahead of me and headed for the door at the far end of the scullery. We barrelled through it at the same time. Duncan kept going down the corridor beyond, but I stopped, trying to lock the door behind us. The handle turned in position, all the way round three hundred and sixty degrees. There was no way to lock the door.

Well, this just keeps getting better and better.

I backed away down the corridor. The door swung open, slowly, revealing the scullery beyond. The undead already filled the room. Unblinking stares looked for fresh meat... and found me.

They shuffled forward. I stabbed with the spear, twice, thrusting deep into dry flesh. The attackers didn't flinch. I thrust again, deep into the belly of a fat thing that had once been a formidable woman. She *sucked* it in, and the spear was torn from my hands. I turned and ran catching up with Duncan in the dining room. He was backing away from the table by the window where four more of the *things* shuffled from their seats. Alive or dead, I didn't know, but it made no difference – they all looked at me with that same *hunger* I was coming to recognise.

"Outside or the stairs?" I heard Duncan say. "They're at the front door already."

"Take the stairs," I said.

Once more we took the stairs almost together, all the way up to the collections room at the top of the building. I slammed the door behind me, but again there was no lock to secure it.

"Shit."

We're trapped.

Outside, footsteps thudded as the undead came up the stairs.

I threw my weight against the door.

"Find something to wedge it. Quick."

I locked out my legs and leaned into the door, trying to put my weight just over the handle. Something heavy hit the other side, hard enough for the door to open by two inches then slam shut again.

Behind me I heard clattering and smashing.

"If you're going to do something, now would be a good time," I shouted.

The door slammed against my shoulder, opening almost three inches this time.

"Let it open further next time," Duncan shouted.

"Open further? Are you mad?"

"Trust me. I have a plan."

The next time the door slammed against me I let it open slightly wider.

Duncan stepped forward and threw something through the gap, something that smashed in the hallway beyond.

I put my shoulder to the door and slammed it shut. This time Duncan helped me.

"Okay," the older man said. "Now I need your lighter."

I managed to dig inside my jacket, came up with the Zippo and handed it to Duncan.

"If I say duck, don't ask 'Where?'" Duncan said.

The door slammed hard on my shoulder. My feet slid on the floor as the door opened, six inches, then nine. A long dry hand at the end of an arm clad in thick blue serge gripped the inside edge and pulled. A head followed, grey hair hanging lankly over a face further obscured by a full salt-and-pepper beard. The blue serge was a heavy jacket, done up with silver buttons.

A naval man.

I heard the distinctive sound of a Zippo being fired up.

"Duck," Duncan shouted.

I ducked. Something flew past my ear, something that burned yellow.

The hall beyond the door exploded into flame. The blue-serge clad figure fell away from the door. I slammed it shut and Duncan wedged a chair under the handle. Even though the door was firmly closed the smell of cooking meat seeped through the gaps.

"Good plan," I said when I'd caught my breath. "What did you use?"

He looked sheepish.

"A bottle of Smirnoff. Blue Label. I hid it up here so the missus wouldn't catch me at it."

That was the first I'd heard of a Mrs. Duncan. I wasn't sure I wanted to ask, but I had to.

"And where is she now?"

He waved at the door, fresh tears in his eyes.

"Out there for all I know. I put her out in the garden nearly a year ago now. But if I know her she'll be up and about – she never missed a chance to give me a hard time."

My phone rang, saving me from having to get deeper into the conversation. It was Doug.

"How's it going?" he asked. In reply he got a thirty-second diatribe on the merits of not splitting up text messages. I may even have used several words my mammy wouldn't have liked very much. Even then, he wasn't particularly contrite, but I couldn't afford the satisfaction of hanging up on him – Doug was our only chance to get out of this.

"Come on then," I said when he showed no signs of replying. "I know you. You wouldn't have phoned if you didn't have something for me."

"McLeod was a naval officer," Doug began.

I didn't have time for the long version. Something had started pounding on the door again, rattling it in hinges that looked old and rusted.

"I know," I said. "I've met the man. Very sprightly, considering he's been dead these many years."

I heard Doug's sharp intake of breath.

"And have you seen the collection?" he finally said.

"Seen it? I'm standing in the middle of it."

I didn't have to see him to know he was smiling.

"That's good," he said. "You need to find her hair."

"Her?"

"Mrs. McLeod. He had her scalp and hair made into a headpiece after she died. There was a great scandal and..."

"Enough," I said, feeling as if I'd just kicked an excited puppy. "Just get to the point Doug. The undead are at the door, and they're worse than the bible-thumpers."

The pounding at the door got louder as if to emphasize my point. The top hinge squealed, the screws starting to loosen in the sockets.

I sensed his smile had faded, but he did speed up.

"It's a talisman," he said. "Part of a Zulu necromancy ritual. It's used in conjunction with..."

"Let me guess... a map written on human skin?"

"Right first time. And now that you've burned one, you have to burn the other. If you don't all those affected by the curse will arise and walk the earth and..."

"Yadda yadda yadda. I've seen the movie," I replied. "Anything else I need to know? Like why this is happening now?"

"Well old McLeod has been in the ground a while now. Maybe this is a last attempt at bringing his wife back before he is too far gone?"

Just at that the door decided it had taken enough of a beating and gave way beneath the assault. The first thing to come through was an arm clad in blue serge – badly singed, still smoking, but unmistakably belonging to McLeod.

"I'll get back to you on that one," I said. I threw the phone aside and tried to put my shoulder against the door. "Find a wig," I shouted at Duncan. "It belongs to his wife."

Then I was too busy to talk for a while.

~-o0O0o-~

It felt like someone was hitting me on the back with a large lump of wood... in fact, someone was. McLeod's hand gripped at the edge of the door and *tugged*. I had to slam my weight back against the door, hard, to keep him out.

Too far gone my arse.

"What exactly am I looking for?" Duncan called.

"How the hell should I know? Just burn anything that looks like hair."

The weight behind me pressed even harder and I buckled. A withered hand grabbed at me, and I had to leave a clump of hair behind as I pulled away. The door fell in with a crash.

"I've found it," Duncan shouted at the same moment.

I had to back away as McLeod came through the doorway, those who had paid for his obsession shuffling close behind.

"You'd better be right wee man," I said. "Quick. Where's the Zippo?"

That was when I remembered.

He threw it out into the corridor.

But hardened nicotine addicts aren't stupid enough to be out without a backup plan. I held McLeod off with one hand and fished a box of matches out of my inside pocked with the other.

McLeod's teeth *clacked* perilously close to my fingers.

I threw the matches in Duncan's direction, hoping he was quick enough to catch them.

Then I was in a fight for my life. McLeod showed no sign of being too far-gone for a fight. He took my best punch, right on the point of the jaw. His head rocked and a split appeared in the skin of his neck, gaping bloodless and gray. It didn't slow him any. He came inside my swinging arm and grabbed me. He forced my head to one side and exposed my neck. Then he sniffed, twice, close together, as if checking my after-shave.

"Where is it!" he said.

His voice was rough, harsh, almost a bark.

I tried to speak, but the grip around my throat was so tight that all I could manage was to keep breathing.

"Where is it!" he said again, almost shouting this time. His breath smelled, of stale food and stagnant water, but I guessed now wasn't a good time to tell him.

With his spare hand he went through my pockets; fast and methodical, like a pro. When he didn't find anything, the hold on my throat tightened further still. I tried to break the grip, but my strength was going fast. I punched him, hard, just below the heart, but he didn't even wince.

He laughed in my face.

"Is that all you've got lad?"

He threw me away, like a discarded rag. His hand barely moved, yet I flew, a tangle of arms and legs, crashing hard against the far wall and falling to a heap on the floor. Something gave way in my lower back; a tearing pain that I knew meant trouble.

I hoped I'd live long enough to see it.

I turned to see him coming for me again. I held up an arm, but in truth I had no fight left in me. McLeod came on, teeth *clacking*.

~~-o0O0o-~~

Duncan saved my life.

Just as McLeod reached for me, his minions right behind him, a forest of arms my only view, I heard Duncan shout.

"Is this what you're looking for?"

McLeod turned away from me, and I had a clear view across the room as the case came to its denouement.

Duncan had what looked like a long wig in his left hand, and a burning candle in his right.

"Burn it," I shouted.

But it looked like I was in no immediate danger. The undead were all focussed on Duncan. Nobody moved, the only sound the sputter of the flickering candle.

"Burn it!" I shouted again.

Duncan had other ideas.

"I know how you feel," he said to McLeod. "Every day, I want her back. Every day I miss her. But look at yourself man. Do you want her back like this? Could you stand it? Here..."

"No!" I shouted, but couldn't stop him handing the wig to McLeod.

"Let her go," Duncan said softly. "Set both of you free."

McLeod didn't move, just stood there stroking the hairpiece as Duncan put the candle under, first the wig, then the navy man's long beard.

He went up like a piece of dry paper, consumed to ash in less time than I would take to smoke a cigarette. At that point I expected the others with him to fall to the ground, or wither and turn to ash themselves.

That's how it works in the movies.

But this was Largs, on a holiday weekend. Things didn't work like in the movies around here. The undead milled around the room, seemingly devoid of purpose, maybe twenty of them in various states of decomposition.

"We should burn these too," I said, but I knew already my heart wasn't in it, and I was glad when Duncan disagreed with me.

"Just leave them to me," he said. "I'll take care of them, like I've always done."

By the time I left he had them all in the dining room, sitting over cups of tea that would never get drunk, fancy teacakes that would never get eaten.

That's Largs for you.

__William Meikle__ is a Scottish writer, now living in Canada, with twenty novels published in the genre press and over 300 short story credits in thirteen countries. - See more at:

http://www.williammeikle.com/#sthash.fpV5roQn.dpuf

13 TO 33
by Ursula Sutter

I was crying myself to sleep over the idea that I would die a virgin. Of course I would die a virgin. My breasts were too big and I only got along with adults. A clock was ticking. Thirteen would become fourteen, and soon I would be eighteen, and then I would go to college where also nobody would want me, and then if I graduated a virgin people would smell it on me, and then I would be forty, and surely nobody wants that, and then I would be fifty and then I would be DEAD. A virgin. A total virgin. I should never have told people I was bisexual. Or have been mean. To boys. Who were so UGH. Or have worn those terrible clothes.

Two years later, in July:

"What did you like and what did you not like?" We are naked on a futon in a garden level, green light bouncing in off the ferns and birch trees. He has big eyes, curly hair, punk music, a foreskin, and a mother who grows pot on the porch and can't take the trash to the dump, so it sits in the woods in plastic bags, waiting for someone with a license.

"I liked when you sucked my nipples, I didn't like your hand pressing the tendon in my groin," I show him the line of my tendon. "What about you? What did you like? What did you not like?" I am happy and calm, the idea that we are having sex for our mutual pleasure delights me. In August he confesses he loves me. I listen to him carefully, considering. A week later I tell him I love him too. There is art I suddenly understand, books and songs. I feel connected. When my parents catch on and ground me, and threaten legal action against him unless I stop having sex with him, I do stop. Unwillingly. Their objections are moral, they say. I'm too young to do what I'm doing. He has turned 18. I won't be 16 for a month. My mother is furious and disappointed. My father is too, and he cries. The email he read he reads out to me in mocking, high pitched, feminine tones

"It's been a week since I've had seeeeeh-ehx," then he looks at me over his glasses, voice becoming deep, serious, sonorous. "You told Rebecca you found out I was looking at porn, and that gave you 'heavy ammunition,' but I am an adult and I'll do what I damn well please." It doesn't occur to me for seventeen years that the doubtful agency of the women in the porn he says he has a right to makes him a hypocrite. They were probably 18. I was 15, but I was his daughter. Emphasis on *his*.

When I was 20, in a hotel in Boston:
    "Why don't you two get it over with and FUCK already?" We look up at the woman lying on the bed, who has been theatrically moaning at having her stupid wrist stroked. We look at each other and practice exchanging wicked grins. I see her teeth when she smiles and I feel a pulse of recognition in my chest. I mistake it for lust, and not for the last time. We kiss on the street in the old combat zone. A man with a shopping cart and a huge coat yells his appreciation of our display.
    We will kiss **performatively** for a few months, look at each other with glee, and snicker, knowingly. We will try sex a few times. It won't be very good. We will both think we aren't as gay as we thought we were. She will dump me for the man she marries and divorces. She will date only women after that.
    We will forever refer to the woman on the bed as Scary Wrist-Moaning Lady. We will be obnoxious in public. We will love each other deeply, and be grateful for our intimacy. I will see her through the revelation that her father raped her when she was an infant. She will see me through the revelation that I sexually assaulted the person who became my wife, the night I first kissed her and touched her no longer erect penis. She will listen to me patiently when I insist that I have unwittingly raped my wife, over and over, during our decade's worth of marital sex.
    She will see me through my subsequent divorce.

In East Asia, I am 32 at home and 34 in this Confucian society:
    "I was suicidal until she showed her hand," I type.

51

"What did she do?" the words pop up on my screen.

"You know the pepper gas thing?" We talk in the shorthand of old friends.

"Yeah, the mace when she cooks?"

"I kept asking her to stop and she says she's sorry but she isn't. The aircon was on because Death Heat, so the windows were closed. She hates the aircon but she let me turn it on because I was miserable and sweating sitting still. Then, once I was comfortable, she had to cook. And it had to be spicy. And she had to make the oil hit the smoke point after the peppers were in. I was coughing and gagging and upset. She said I had no right to complain because she 'was uncomfortable for all of our marriage,' "

"Woah. That's crazy."

"Yeah. I didn't even get angry, I just shut the door in her face and opened the window in the bedroom."

"…"

"Everything crystalized."

"Yeah. You said everything crystalized. But you hadn't said why."

"That was it. I knew she would have said anything to get out of our marriage. It didn't matter what the truth was."

"Is it ok to say I am having a dance party in my head right now? Cause I am."

"Yeah, no problem. You aren't the only one." I can see her smile and her teeth in my head. All the way over in East Asia.

In Boston again for a visit, in another hotel, and I am 33:

"Oh, let me help you," and she zips my dress back up over the tattoo that I got after my wife left me. Which is why we came to the hotel that her two fiancés have checked into, because you can't take the woman you have been dating for fourteen years into the bathroom of the kosher deli to show her the single magpie that now covers your back. Not when she keeps kosher, has a rabbi father and hasn't kissed you in years. But especially not after she tells you that Jews can't get tattoos.

We sit on one of the beds to talk more. It is high and the edges are curved, it feels a little dangerous. I shift to the middle, looking for a steady perch. "Can I ask you a question I've been dying to ask you for years?" she sounds hesitant.

"Of course!"

"Can I touch you?" I look in her eyes

"I would love it if you touched me," I say, clearly and softly, and place the back of my hand on hers.

"I didn't think I could, when you got engaged. And I was afraid to ask,"

"I didn't want to push you. And you offered to break up with me a couple years ago, but I didn't want to. Breaking up felt wrong, and saying we were dating wasn't hurting anyone,"

"Oh, thank G-d." We laugh. "I mean, we don't have to have sex right now or anything,"

"I know," I say, and embrace her.

We are standing when I kiss her lips. I remember their shape from before. "Your lips were always so soft," she says. I am slightly taller than her, and I cup her face, her back, her breasts. It's strange to be the one leading. To push my desire out into my arms and fingers and lips so I can act with intention and tenderness.

"Is this ok?" I breathe.

"Yes, and you don't have to keep asking,"

"But I do, for me," I explain. "she says I raped her for a decade, I have to ask. For my sanity," she kisses me and runs her nails across my back. I arch and moan, surprising myself. My skin is hungry. "I want to take this all off, I didn't bring extra underpants,"

"I want to take mine off too," so we step apart and take our clothes off, laying them over a chair so they won't wrinkle, grinning at each other's feminine practicality.

She crawls up the bed first, her breasts and bottom full and womanly and soft. The bed is soft and pale, and she is soft and pale. The feminist fist tattoo on my left shoulder is the only dark thing I can see. Everything feels good and I try to notice everything. I look into her eyes and smile, I lick her neck and smile, I curl my fingers into her warm and gentle cunt and smile.

"Ok?" I ask, and start to rub with intention.

"Yes," she says, and the blush spreads up her chest.

"I'm glad I cut my nails,"

"I didn't cut mine."

"Yeah, the ride's a little rough. Try rubbing my clit instead?"

"You're as soft as I remember,"

"You too."

Later, she wants to go down on me. She hasn't, but she wants to now. She is hesitant at first, not sure how to avoid getting hair in her mouth, surprised I smell different than I did ten years ago.

There is a knock. I hope it is her future husbands, I'd like to meet the one I haven't met yet. But it's the maids who have come to de-feather the room. Her fiancés have requested hypo-allergenic bedding because she is allergic to goose down. The maids say they can't come back later. She puts her clothes on to let them in. I hide in the bathroom and listen to the maids giggling. Right before they leave, they suggest she use the 'Do Not Disturb' sign. I open the bathroom door and take her, red faced, into my arms. It's time for me to go. We shower, she takes the antibiotic she always has to take after sex.

At the apartment where my boyfriend and girlfriend live, on the same visit to Boston:

"Then the maids came to de-feather the room!"

"Oh no!"

"It was sad. But it was almost time for me to go anyway," I tell her.

He is asleep, we are allowed to wake him up in two hours. There is a cat in my lap. There is a cat on the back of the sofa. There is a cat in the chair. There is a cat picking its way across the mantle in front of the Yule Log T.V. show streaming in from Netflix. She is the most talkative I have ever seen her, and she tells me about therapy and why she stopped drinking. About how the new meds are working for her. About how the new meds are working for him. It has changed their lives, the new medicine. His chronic and rare disease is diagnosed and under control for the first time ever. They aren't going from crisis to crisis. She tells me about how that change is stressful, because they finally have time to deal with the stress that has accumulated for five years. They finally have time to deal with how their lives have changed.

I stroke the side of her face and she closes her eyes, leaning into my caress. Her neck is tiny, thinner than my bicep. The collar I bought her still closes at the smallest grommet. We kiss. I think that I want to ask her if I can take her clothes off. I realize I can ask her if I can take her clothes off, and also that I have to ask her if I can take her clothes off. I remember that odd sensation with my other girlfriend: I have to push my desire into my limbs, I have to push myself into action. It's so different with women. Men, men are easy.

"I want to take your clothes off, but will your other roommate come home?"

"He shouldn't, but I'll chain the door in case." We stand, I dump a cat out of my lap. I take my cardigan off. She comes back from the front door and I put my arms around her shoulders, leaning down to kiss her. Her lips are as soft as mine. I take her shirt off, roughly.

"Ok?"

"Yeah," she's leaning into my hands. I pick her up to hear her gasp and slowly walk her back to the couch, not able to see my feet and not trusting the cats. I set her down and kneel between her knees, pulling her pants off. Her boots are still on, we take them off and I see her hot pink, fuzzy socks.

"Socks off or on?"

"Off is ok," I strip them off and see her butterfly tattoo. I push her knees wide, and look into her eyes.

"Yeah?"

"Oh, yeah." I push my shoulders into the backs of her thighs and start to lick her cunt. On my knees, still dressed, right hand two fingers deep, I realize that shoulders against the backs of thighs is a good piece of advice for how to eat pussy. Hair in your mouth to be expected is another piece of advice. Make circles with your tongue. The more you suck the clit the bigger it can get...

I lose the thread of my list of advice, and I just I close my eyes and suck her inside me, over and over. I reach up and take a breast in my hand, nipple barely spilling out past my thumb. She can take more here than she used to, or so her husband has told me. I look at her face. It's pink and open. I pull and squeeze her breast carefully while I mash her clit. I can feel her start to flutter around the knuckles I have inside her. I watch her cum. I kiss my way up her belly.

"Hello, darling."

"Hi," she giggles. I put my wet fingers in her mouth and she moans, lapping them. I trace her lips.

"Should we wake him up?"

"Yeah…" She wraps herself in a scarf and we go into their bedroom. She touches his shoulder and says his name. He wakes up looking confused and angry, but she laughs at him mischievously.

"Hey, stranger." He looks at me, and I see the recognition when it happens.

"Hi," he smiles at me with love, and affection, and my chest fills with sadness. The last time I saw him, he was sicker than he let on. Every time I leave, I do it in the knowledge that I might not see him again. But maybe that is over. Maybe he'll stay healthy this time. He looks good. His hair is shorter, it suits him.

"Scoot up," I say, and he pulls up his legs and I sit next to him. Then I hug him. Then I kiss him.

"You taste like pussy?"

"Sorry to break it to you like this, but I've been fucking your wife on the couch for the last hour." He looks at her, wrapped in nothing but her scarf. She giggles. He smiles at her fondly. I kiss him more. "Yup, got started without cha. Cause you're a vampire."

"That's our word! Only people with hemophilia can say that!" He mimics outrage. I kiss his neck, and start to suck gently. He moans.

"Missed you, love."

"Oh, I missed you." He tucks me under his arm. I feel better than I've felt in years.

Later, I spank her ass bright red while he stuffs fingers in her mouth. Then we re-teach her how to fuck a woman with a strap on. He fists me while she kisses me and tries biting my nipples. He fucks

56

me bare, with his own cock, and cums inside me. I smile so much my face aches.

Two weeks later, in a vegetarian diner, days before I have to fly back:
"I heard them tell her to use the 'Do Not Disturb' sign next time. She was RED when I opened the door,"
"That is really funny!" my ex-wife says.
"It was! But I didn't meet the new guy,"
"Too bad,"
"Yeah. And we talked about how we didn't have sex but also about how we failed to talk about not having sex. She thought I was off limits because I was married. And I noticed that the way she related to me changed. I didn't want to push her, because I'm always really careful with women,"
"Yeah," my ex-wife cuts me off and I am suddenly still. We have been so close, as close as you can be to someone who's made you cry yourself to sleep at night. I don't want to be an enemy to the woman I spent ten years with. I don't want any enemies. I drink some beer. She drinks some vegan milkshake.
"So, I think we made that judge's day."
"We did! I was reading about how it's usually women who work in the lower courts. And it seems like it would be like working in a hospice. Like, nobody ever gets better."
"Nobody ever gets something they are really happy about in their court. Justice might be served."
"Right. They might smile, but it would be with grim satisfaction."
"Exactly," and just like that, we are finishing each other's thoughts again. Connected. Talking about how the judge who divorced us was surprised when we started smiling huge and relieved grins. How the whole courtroom cracked up when we high-fived at the end of our hearing. Divorced. Finally.

Ursula Sutter: *It's always the quiet ones*

TUPPERWARE PARTY
by Andy de Fonseca

Edith May Fanny del Mora straightened the shiny pink tablecloth upon which her products were so tediously set up and displayed. She brushed down her mauve cotton skirt-suit and turned her Sales Leader of the Month pin to sit correctly on her lapel. Her carefully painted fingernails lifted the curls of her bobbed hair, which framed a gentle, aged face. Her pale blue eyes were aglow with excitement as they stared out at the small crowd of elderly women taking their seats for the presentation. Edith's smile was warm, welcoming, and genuine, and the laughter lines around her thin lips showed she earned those wrinkles.

"Thank you so much for inviting me into your home, my dear Gertrude," Edith said to the white-haired woman with a purple shawl. Her voice was soft and sweet, as any grandmothers' should be. "God bless you and your hospitality." She paused as the women softly clapped for their hostess. "Ladies," she continued, "my products are here to make your life easier. I'm sure we all have stopped in the middle of cooking and thought to ourselves how much we could really use one of these at the moment." She gestured to her products lined up behind her. "A dinner at the in-laws would have been so much easier if you had simply brought one along." The women chuckled in agreement. "Lord knows we don't have to worry about that at our age, but I always have one in my handbag just in case a situation arises."

Edith picked up the first product. "This adorable little piece is the Shokushu Fakku." She flipped a tiny switch on the bottom and it came alive: eight lime green tentacles, each a foot long, began spinning violently around the power pole Edith held, and vibrated so fiercely the loose skin on her hand shook. "Translated to English, the Tentacle Fuck." She smiled at the crowd, whose presbyopic eyes looked upon it enviously. "This little guy should be inserted into the vagina or anus *before* turning it on. This way, once you flip this switch, the tentacles are already in there, ready to wet your pussy." She giggled. "Goodness. It makes my dentures chatter!" The women laughed adoringly and Edith turned the Tentacle Fuck off. She delicately placed it on the table and picked up the next item.

"This next one you'll want to lube up your hand and lower arm in order to easily put on. Can I get a volunteer?" Hands lifted into the air and she smiled at a greyed woman with faded red hair. With a gleeful smile the woman lifted herself with her cane and limped over. "Just rub this jelly all over my arm, dear. Yes, like that. God bless you, you're an expert. A hand for our volunteer." The red-haired granny snorted a laugh as she bowed to the applause and sat down. Edith shoved her arm into a long, black leather glove, making sure her aged, saggy skin wasn't tugged uncomfortably. Once fully on, she held up her arm to show the end of her hand was fit into a bulbous fisting mitten. It was the size of a bowling ball yet she showed no signs of difficulty with the weight. "This will really get him riled," she squeaked with a twinkle in her eye. "After you say your Lord's Prayer in the evening, just pull out this baby and you'll have no problem finding that prostate of his. Shit and cum will fly from fan to wall so I recommend double-checking on your amount of Tide and baking soda!" The women went to their order forms to take notes. "And you *must* remember - be sure to wash after every rectal insertion before transferring to the vajay. That's just an unnecessary trip to the gynecologist!"

The women nodded and scribbled down notes as Edith removed the hand bulb.

"Ms. del Mora," a sweet, baby-faced fossil chimed in a cracked voice, "what was the name of that product?"

"The Ass Annihilator, love," she smiled. "Column two, section one, fourth item down." She moved to the next product. "This one will need some setup, as you can see." Edith carefully put together a saddle chair with overhanging poles, and several buzzing vibrators strapped on different parts. "This is the No Hole Left Behind seat," she said proudly. "Usually I ask for a volunteer, but you all are dressed so nicely in your church clothes." Every hand in the room went up and Edith's cheery laugh reminded everyone of homemade apple pie. "All right, dear, you can come up." As the geriatric volunteer removed her clothes, Edith carefully folded each piece and put them aside. "You'll notice as she sits down, this big purple shlong will fill her panty hamster, this bulb back here will pop right into her chocolate starfish, and this little suction cup can be adjusted to fit right over her sugared almond." The woman, bare as the baby Jesus, moaned through the few teeth she had left and Edith moved the sucker onto her wrinkled, ashen bean. "Right, so she's good and nestled on the bottom, let's move to the top." Her hands moved to the various-sized toys around the head of white, brittle hair. "This big black aboriginal is for your mouth, of course. It's a good foot long and expects a good deep throat. The more you gag the harder it gets!" The volunteer gagged as if on cue, and gave an arthritic thumbs up. "Remove your hearing aids and these two up here will ear-fuck you until next Tuesday. The two here in front get shoved up your nostrils and swirl around. Only a frontal lobotomy will tickle your brain like this! And these last two are for your tear ducts. They complete the cranial region for a full, vibrating head fucking that travels to your tuna taco with a sour cream ending!"

The elderly women in the room gasped in delight as they watched the volunteer get raw-dogged in every way possible, moaning, groaning, gyrating, jowls twitching, dripping saliva and squirting onto the carpet below her.

"The No Hole Left Behind also comes with an expansion pack!" Edith said, and added another vibrator on the front. "This Cyprian scepter goes right between your bouncing Buddhas for a jolly good time!" She pushed a small button on the bottom and sure enough the floppy flute quaked between the volunteer's Gerber servers. The old woman's sagging tits flopped like two socks caught in a windstorm. "Some like to lay a towel or tarp underneath, some like the stain as a trophy reminder!"

Pens flew across order forms.

"Thank you to our wonderful volunteer!" Edith turned off and pulled away the pulsating toys covered in fluids and helped the woman to her feet. Her knees shook and she almost tripped.

"Whoopsy daisy! Don't want to break a hip, now. There you go, God bless your soul."

As the volunteer put her clothes back on, Edith moved on. "This one I'll demonstrate myself as I'll be using my own little helper." She lifted her cotton skirt and unbuckled her garters, letting her nylons fall to the floor. She slipped off her frilly granny-panties and stood with her legs spread. Reaching behind her, she pulled a small chihuahua out of its carrier case. "This is my little angel, Malkovich. He has helped me with this demonstration countless times. Say hello, Malkovich." She waved his paw and the floral pattern-wearing women cooed. Edith once again reached behind her and grabbed a rod. "This item is for the brave souls who have seen it all and want something exciting before their nightly pudding! All you do is stick your little pooch on like so-" Edith rammed the rod into Malkovich's tiny chihuahua ass hole and there was a shrill yelp from the dog. "And place it inside like so-" She spread her varicose-veined legs even further, reached under, and shoved dog and rod inside her ninety-year-old drooping meat wallet. "And flip the switch." With a flick of her finger, there was a loud vibrating, followed by muffled barking. "And there you have it," she smiled as her hips moved back and forth. Her hand held firmly onto the rod despite the two tiny doglegs that stuck out her snatch, wriggling to get free. "Any questions?"

A plump lady with thick glasses raised her hand. "Couldn't you do that one without the rod, deary? And are cats just as well?"

Edith smiled as she held the dog-rod in place. "I don't recommend it without the rod as the vibrations help your twinkie filling come, which eases the pooch into your cootch. And any animal should do fine so long as it's yours or you have permission from a friend to use theirs. Fantastic question, love." Edith removed the chihuahua, now soaked in her expired baby batter and smelling of mothballs, KY jelly, and shellfish. His bulged eyes were wide in horror and shook even after the rod was turned off. "All right, ladies. Time for the nasty stuff you'll need to go to confessional for!"

The grannies squealed and readied their pens.

Andy de Fonseca *is author of* The Cheat Code for God Mode, *some historical essay published in a college book, and various short stories in anthologies. She still enjoys Cheez Its, and is still the coordinator for the Chicago branch of* The Planetary Society. *She most recently became the co-creator of a womb parasite, which should be published beginning March 2016. If you'd like to learn more about Andy, visit her website at www.andylikesyou.com.*

TOMOGU WILL HAVE VENGEANCE
by Andrew Coulthard

Tomogu's dark eyes gazed across the table at Miika, her raven hair falling in silky cascades to either side of a fine featured, olive-skinned face.

"So, what now?" she asked softly. When he didn't answer she took up a slice of spiced quince from the platter between them and slipped the fruit crescent between her full lips, chewing slowly.

Miika sat perfectly still, wine goblet halfway to his mouth. He was handsome in a rugged fashion: tall and broad-shouldered, with a square, clean-shaven jaw, short auburn hair and smouldering blue eyes.

For a time they sat thus, eyes locked, until Miika broke away from her gaze, glancing around the dimly lit tent and breathing deeply of the scented air. She smiled to herself; he was unnerved by her.

She rose in a single motion and walked to the centre of the tent, loose silken robes flowing about her. Sensing his eyes on her she turned to face him, a smile playing at the corners of her mouth.

"Shall we cement our alliance?" she asked softly.

Miika swallowed. He couldn't find his voice. Taking a mouthful of wine he cleared his throat.

"Isn't that what we're doing," he asked and nodded at the food and wine on the table.

By way of reply Tomogu extinguished the candles one by one until the only light came from a brazier of glowing coals. Then, turning away again, she shrugged off her robe, the lines and curves of her body an interplay of flesh and shadow.

"Come," she said and vanished through the curtain to the sleeping area.

Trembling slightly, Miika rose to his feet and strode after her, casting off his clothing as he went.

Beyond the heavy hanging darkness was complete.

"Tomogu," he whispered.

Suddenly she was there, the flesh of her breasts and belly pressing against him, her lips on his chest. He felt himself hardening. Tomogu enclosed the shaft of his cock in slender fingers and he let out a gasp.

"Love me," she purred, leading him further into the darkness.

They bumped against the edge of the bed and she released him, clambering onto the thick heap of mattresses.

"Tomogu," he whispered again, voice quivering with lust.

"I'm here," she replied from the dark.

She sensed him climb onto the bed, his strong hands groping across the blanket in search of her. They found her feet first, massaging the soles and heels before moving upward to stroke her ankles and the soft curves of her calves. Her breathing quickened and with a grunt Miika stooped to kiss the flesh of her legs with savage passion, his lips and breath hot on her skin as they worked their way up the inside of her thighs. When at last he reached the moist flesh of her mound she tensed, holding her breath in anticipation. But Miika paused, breathing deeply of her perfumed musk, his lips barely brushing against her sex.

She waited for what felt an eternity, breath coming in short gasps, her body tense. Then without warning his tongue darted into her slit and he began licking back and forth from the opening of her cunt to her swollen clitoris.

Tomogu fell back against the pillows, groaning with pleasure.

"In me," she moaned, grabbing his shoulders and wrenching his muscular frame over her.

Supporting himself on one arm he guided his thick cock to her moist opening. They groaned in unison as he pushed his entire length into her.

"Yes, Miika, yes" she sighed, clutching at his back while he thrust in and out.

"Tomogu," he moaned in response.

"Harder, *faster!*" she panted squirming and arcing her back.

He hammered into her, muscles standing out in knots and ridges while she thrashed about beneath him, her curves glistening in the darkness.

"Oh, oh, ohhhh yessss," she cried.

Miika thrust harder still, grunting each time he penetrated her until Tomogu thrust upwards with her crotch, grabbing his backside and pulling him to her with all her strength. Giving out a long cry she climaxed, her body shuddering against his and moments later Miika came inside her, all the tension draining from his body.

With a long contented moan he rolled over and flopped down onto the bed.

"Alliance cemented," he breathed.

Tomogu chuckled softly, gentle aftershocks of pleasure still passing through her lower belly. She was about to tell him that it wouldn't be cemented until morning, but lights appeared beyond the curtain.

"What?!" she breathed. "I gave orders we were not to be disturbed."

The curtain was ripped aside and burning brands were thrust towards them in a dazzling glare. Before Tomogu fully realised what was going on Miika had leapt at their attackers in a confusion of flames, flailing fists and shouting. In moments he vanished from sight beneath the whirling brands and fire had taken hold of the hangings and carpet.

She couldn't save him.

Darting under the cloth hanging at the rear of her bed, Tomogu entered into the area of her tent where she kept clothing and weapons. She fumbled in the darkness, dragging a woollen tunic over her head and drawing her curved sword from its scabbard. Then with a sweep of the blade she slashed an opening in the outer cloth of the tent and stepped out into the night.

In the camp beyond chaos reigned. Scores of men armed with spears, clubs and axes were running to and fro. They were not her men. The strangers wore baggy, loose-fitting clothes and leather hoods obscuring their faces. Many gathered around the low tents in which her men were sleeping, dousing them in oil and setting them alight. When her terrified followers burst yelling into the night they were knocked down and hacked to pieces.

Tomogu was famed for her skill with a blade, but she stood no chance alone against so many. She cast about her for an escape route, but there seemed to be enemy warriors and slaughter everywhere. Sneaking around her tent into the shadows she dashed from tent to tent toward the edge of the camp where the horses were tethered in a low stone enclosure. However, at the entrance to the enclosure her guards lay dead and a half dozen enemy warriors were looting their bodies. Beyond them, frightened animals stamped and whinnied, straining at their tethers.

Tomogu gave the warriors a wide birth making her way to the rear of the enclosure. Once there she paused ensuring nobody had seen her then she clambered over the low heap of stones and made her way to her mount, Kujoko.

Whispering to calm him, she stroked his forehead and patted his thick muscular neck. Then she loosened the tether rope and used it to make an improvised bridle. A glance told her that the warriors at the corral entrance still hadn't seen her; they were arguing over some piece of loot.

She watched them briefly, committing the details of their appearance to memory. Her men were all dead or soon would be; Miika was almost certainly dead too along with all of his followers. And the wealth that had taken her years to amass, coin, silver and horses, was now in the hands of these warriors.

"If I survive this night there'll be a reckoning," she vowed under her breath. Then she led Kujoko from the enclosure, clambered up onto his bare back and galloped off into the night.

Andrew Coulthard first saw the light of day on the wind-lashed eastern coast of Northumbria. He then spent most of his childhood and youth in the western shadow of the highland boundary fault. Since 1990 he has dwelt north of the land of the Geats - where it can get very cold.

When not writing he spends time with his family, explores heroic landscapes and enjoys surfeits of good food and drink - sometimes all at once.

THE LOW SPARK OF HIGHBROW PORN
by Jess Gulbranson

In looking at poetry and song titles for a denotative meaning-anything goes. Film and comic titles are little more straightforward. There are a few that are needlessly arcane, but not as a general rule. Once we reach the domain of pornography, however, things are different. Porn titles are not like those of mainstream movies- their content, as related to the subject matter they signify, is more direct than in that of any other medium.

Transsexual Seduction. Cum On Her Face. World's Largest Gangbang. There is not much wiggle room, so to speak, for a guess on what these films are going to be about. Imagine if we were able to apply such a reductionist process to other areas. In a recent discussion with a colleague, the idea was floated that all competitive sports could be retitled "Ball Direction." Given the homoerotic nature of those sports, one might be forgiven for thinking that this could, without much modification, be a porn title itself. This pure expression of the *ding-an-sich* and its manifestation in denominative discourse might, depending on one's critical perspective, be refreshing or disgusting. Why, we must ask, is this practice so consistent for the medium? They are a reflection of the movies they signify.

Before the advent of the internet, porn had come to fulfil a trend of distilling the art of erotica into "strictly business". Compilation tapes and discs attempted to cram as many thematically-related scenes, removing all trace of narrative in service of providing as much plain stimulation as possible. Remember this- it will be important later. This process was not driven out of any sort of artistic choice- in fact, during this period, apart from a few creators who maintained branding identity, the concept of "director-as-auteur" had all the appearances of vanishing from this subset of the cinematic arts.

It was the demand of the market that pushed porn into a state of skeletal minimalism. When adult movies made their transition to rentals and arcades, the viewers- and the content suppliers up the chain- demanded immediate gratification. Time is money, especially in the video booth.

This commodification was itself later greeted with a rejection. On the positive side, it inspired a new generation of filmmaker to create such artistic abstractions as *Beautiful Agony*, or the genderqueer inclusivity of the *Crashpad* series, examples of how porn should be-focused on pleasure, gratification, and mutual enjoyment. It also inspired the "casting" and "gonzo" styles, subgenres focused on humiliation, degradation, and brutality, and none of those in any sort of artistic context that would put them anywhere even close to a healthy expression of sexuality or competent artistry. Interestingly enough, these negative subgenres seem to step backwards by adding *more* non-sex parts, poorly-acted plotless dialogues that serve only as a setup, not for anything truly erotic, but for a higher level of verisimilitude in service of greater humiliation for its actresses.

It hasn't always been like this, however. Erotic cinema- from its advent in the early days of film itself, up to the rise of the videotape-was just that: cinema. Porn started simply as a type of film that contained risque nudity and unsimulated sex, and was focused on the erotic. While the continuity, production values, or quality of acting may have slipped, they were at least there in the first place, and attempts were made to sustain a substantive creative effort. The role of director was key when porn was chic, and not solely the domain of the ruthless editor. There was room in the pornographic oeuvre for fun, for experimentation, as shown in features with such nonindicative names as *Behind The Green Door* and *The Opening Of Misty Beethoven*. As we've discussed, this was not to last, but a few enclaves of creativity remained, and it is one of these that brings us here today...

Midget In A Suitcase.

This film, from 2000 when the internet's stranglehold on porn had nowhere to go but up, is a bit of high concept that originated not in a hastily-named cashgrab compilation, but in a fantasy of

Bridget Powers, the film's star. Powers- the titular midget- often dreamed as a girl that she might find a partner who was himself very small, and imagined a little man who might pop out of a suitcase to romance her. It was this idea, inverted to feature Powers herself, that was the genesis of *Midget In A Suitcase*. Highbrow porn had certainly been attempted along the way in the days since porn's Golden Age, but usually only by grafting a simple plot or theme onto the scenes of hardcore sex- a pale imitation of the days of *Misty Beethoven*. Powers also envisioned *Suitcase* as an old-fashioned silent film. This was somewhat lost in the execution, for while there is certainly no dialogue, the sounds of diegetic fucking are in evidence, with no musical accompaniment.

Suitcase begins with a protracted opening sequence of a large man lugging a suitcase through a neighborhood that has seen better days. On first viewing I couldn't help but hear the theme to *Midnight Cowboy*. An elegiac tone to this introductory scene undoubtedly supports this fancy, and one could imagine many different songs used here to enhance the plaintive mood: "Tangled Up In Blue," perhaps, or "Try A Little Tenderness", or even "Driving Your Girlfriend Home" if a measure of irony is allowed. Once the man arrives at his destination, he carries the burden upstairs to a strange, lonely room. Some compilations omit everything up to this entrance and describe the scene a man on a work retreat at a swanky resort smuggling his girlfriend in. There was never a resort in a neighborhood so desolate, and most hotel rooms do not resemble some weirdo's hastily evacuated garret apartment. Of course, once the suitcase is opened on the bed, only a brief scene of Powers jumping for joy separates the narrative from its expected praxis. Before this commences, there are smiles all around and this seems to be a guiding element from Powers' *weltanschaung*- that sex is about fun and feeling good, and that Powers herself is a beautiful woman whose sexuality exists entirely outside the midget category.

Powers neither distances herself from or minces words about her status, though in interviews she certainly addresses a level of interconnectedness that would satisfy the Tathagatha, or even Gregory Bateson. This first scene is itself unremarkable- the male actor is about as loving as it gets in the business, and Powers is indeed beautiful and seems to enjoy herself. Three of out of four of the film's scenes follow this suitcase-to-sex formula. The second scene of the film is a curious aversion- the girl featured is neither a midget or in a suitcase, and her sad and workmanlike performance is a far cry from Powers' delicious vitality. It is this counterexample that points us to the heart of this movie's strength. It's not any particular fetishistic notion about the novelty of dwarf sex, or even the absurdist conceit of the suitcase itself, but the presence of a strong, charismatic woman commanding the respect and desire of her colleagues and audience with a combination of her primary performance and her honesty and articulation as evidenced in the paratext. In porn, a genre whose content often runs alone by dint of practicality and prurience, there is very little paratext available apart from interviews, and it might easily be argued that this has no bearing on an evaluation of the piece in question. It is this reviewer's position that in matters of critical significance, context is king. Powers' statements regarding her significant input in the creative process, in this film and others, hint at a gender parity that slips beyond any third-wave notions of sex-positive feminism. Her willingness to bend the potentially controversial tropes regarding her dwarfism, and willingness through personal agency and significant maturity to balk the expectation that midget porn only exists as a sort of outlet for repressed hebephilia, maintain this. Despite the occasional costume including a tiara or wings, and the magical realism of *Suitcase*, Bridget Powers is not an elf, or fairy, or little girl.

Mentions of mythological creatures are perhaps appropriate, as *Midget In A Suitcase* seems to already be passing into legend. Only 13 years old, the video is out of print, which is perfectly normal for a reasonably obscure porn title, but this is the age of the Internet. Almost any pornographic video is available for free, and indeed scenes from *Suitcase* are easily found, though like almost all of these free clips have been trimmed down to a bare minimum of pertinent fucking. Thus, without the opening scenes I have mentioned, the elegiac quality of *Suitcase* is lost, and the paratextual assertions of its star are found only by a truly ergodic exertion of research. The non-porn scenes themselves can only be found with a Herculean- or perhaps Tantalean- effort.

This is an unfortunate consequence of an egalitarian internet- why would one suffer the wooden narrative scenes- asserted by Mark Leyner as being an 8th amendment violation- when there is time and bandwidth on the line? Most viewers of porn arrive not to parse the works in an aesthetic sense, but to jack off. A similar phenomenon exists with video services such as Youtube- where funny individual lines, the "best parts", are preserved apart from their source. Mainstream media at least have the luxury of cultural and entrepreneurial preservation in the public scope. Mention of *Midget In A Suitcase* occurs infrequently on message boards and the like, but usually in the vaguely nostalgic tones reserved for half-remembered schoolyard dirty jokes. The orphaned erotic scenes will continue to haunt the tubes of the world's networks for the foreseeable future, but without their context within a larger work, their impact- and indeed the film's artistic identity itself- will be lost. It is the opinion of this reviewer that any further diminishment of such an absurdist classic as *Midget In A Suitcase* into obscurity would be a damnable shame.

Jess Gulbranson is an author, artist, critic, and composer. At his most recent public appearance, he and coauthor Garrett Cook had an audience feed their mana to an egregore called "Tony Shrapnel". Current projects include children's books, a grimoire, and the unofficial Dark Souls *manga.* He lives in Portland with his wife and daughters, where he was recently ordained as a Buddhist priest.

WHITE EYELET
by Anna Suarez

As I see I've spilled
huckleberry jam on
white eyelet, you take
my thigh, sink your teeth
into my flesh.

I know of the tulips in your yard,
Your hand-rolled French cigarettes.

Dr. Ramos says
"manic depressive"
and purses her lips.

I watch cars go by,
inhaling deeply,
lungs swollen to
the size of birds
because I want
to breathe this
entire city
in.

There are strands
of my hair, & drops
of perfume oil in
your bed.

I tell myself I am strands
of black hair, rose oil, in
a kingdom where castles
are hewn of raindrops,
patiently expecting
the Great Flood.

Anna Suarez *is a poet from New Jersey, currently based in Portland,
Oregon. Her work explores intimacy, the feminine experience, eroticism,
and mental illness. She is currently working on her bachelors in
philosophy and french at Portland State University. Her future creative
projects include a book of poetry and a memoir.*

DEJIA
by Jon R. Meyers

The constant hum and of Kyuss Valley hissed in the dormant electronic skies outside of the Mushi Complex. The walls of the complex were paper-thin and there was almost an art in one keeping the demons of the valley out. These demons consisted of miscellaneous and ragged street thugs, jagged pimps and drug craving bimbo-esque mechanical prostitutes and showgirls. Crime was at an all-time high in Kyuss Valley.

Dejia knew this. She cleverly burrowed herself inside of an old electron box that sat mid-wall on level six of the Mushi Complex. Inside of the box led to a hole in the wall beneath a few active straggling wires; in which it wasn't uncommon to produce a spark from time to time. Beyond that, led to a tight quarter somewhere between the walls and beneath the air ducts of the complex. This is where Dejia had been living for the past six months. This box, at one-time, when active, controlled the parameters of the entire city.

The city of Kyuss Valley was a vast and spoiled metropolis of lost hope and broken dreams.

This was a place where Mecha Girls went to die.

Dejia, like the other Mecha Girls, moved to Kyuss Valley in an attempt to hit it big. Kyuss Valley was once a place of magic and fame. This is why a large number of these mechanical Angelbots drifted to such a place. However, Kyuss Valley was definitely not the same as it once was. Sadness had started to linger and take over.

Everything had changed after the war.

Kyuss Valley was initially taken over by a group of street thugs by the name of "The Anodes." The Anodes were led by a man by the name of Mr. Ducati. Mr. Ducati was a tall, lanky man with a patch over his left-eye. It was rumored that he'd been attacked by a group of Droidbots and survived. They turned him inside out and fed him chunks of his own body parts, and still lived to tell the tale. Rumor had it; he then killed a whole fucking slew of those glitchy bastards with his bare hands. Eventually, a group of computer hackers had caught wind of The Anodes and their motives and teamed up with them, too. After these two teams of misfits allied in an attempt to shut the entire city down- they did just that. They were more powerful than ever now.

Kyuss Valley in a matter of six months or so became a place of filth. A place of hopeless refuge. A place where these starving mechanical angels and their precious little patchwork wings went to solicit their hot bodies for sex and pleasure. A place where erect business men held large amounts of cash flow for the prior. Sex and angel trafficking were among two of the largest incomes in the entire city. This is how Kyuss Valley now operated under the command of Mr. Ducati and The Anodes.

Dejia awoke as she heard a large crash in the air duct above her. "Shit, they must have found me," she thought to herself, as she shuffled a few belongings together, shoved them into her messenger bag, placed it over her broken wings, and hit her head on the top of her hiding box on the way out.

Dejia was being chased.

Mr. Ducati and his Anodes were after Dejia. Dead or alive; they needed her. She was one of the few Mecha Girls even left in Kyuss Valley. She was worth big money. She was also a threat to them. She knew too much. One thing that Mr. Ducati didn't know- was that, Dejia was inevitably and currently worthless to him.

Dejia had lost her sex-drive. It'd been hi-jacked.

Without her sex-drive, Dejia's time was numbered. She couldn't take on new clients, and without clients, she'd be flat broke. Without money in Kyuss Valley, she'd be left for fucking dead. Mr. Ducati and his group of cyber hackers would have their way with her and kick her to the curb; her wings scattered into a million pieces along the broken pavement of Kyuss Valley, in the cold, in the dark, her long black electronic hair soaked in gallons of semen and blood... it was just a matter of time.

Dejia ran for the steep, curvy stairwell of the Mushi Complex a few feet in front of her. She could hear a couple of Mr. Ducati's men above her. It sounded like a few floors up.

She hopped up onto the wooden banister and slid down, tight black plastic pants squeaking as she quickly approached level three.

"There she is!" Two of Mr. Ducati's men in black suits screamed from the fourth floor as they fired two shots at her. They had guns. They *always* had guns.

Dejia was just a soft blur in their manic pupils. By the time the two men hit the third floor, she'd already made her way out into the street.

"Fuck! Where'd she go?" They motioned in unison towards the front door, confused.

Dejia took a moment to catch her breath. Her heartbeat paced fast. Her anxieties ran amok within the dark digital confines of Kyuss Valley.

Dejia thought about where to go. She thought about what she should do next. She thought about who would be petty enough to steal her sex-drive. She'd thought at first, perhaps, Mr. Ducati or one of his men were behind it. But the more she thought about all of it, the more she realized- why would Mr. Ducati even want it? For one he was rich and famous. And for two, it was useless to him. He needed her. Dejia knew that he and his men wanted her for her mechanics; her wings, her body and all for her precise and accurate pleasure skills. Dejia was the best at what she did. But why would they want her sex-drive? It couldn't be them. It wasn't them. But then, who?

Dejia signaled for a cyber-cab and made her way over to Mye's flat.

Dejia sat inside of the cab feeling useless. Without her sex-drive, Dejia was lost. She could feel the liquid inside of her pulsing through her CORE suit. Her mechanics moaned and ached for pleasure. But, with her vaginal port lacking the drive- Dejia inevitably had no motive; no drive. She was like a broken anchor in a sea of piss and shit. She'd imagined the moment of being plugged back in, that overall conception of lust and beauty swirling inside of her. Her body being consumed and ravaged by whomever, this is what Dejia lived for now. She needed it. She missed it more than one could ever imagine. If anyone could make her feel better- it was Mye.

The cab pulled up outside of Mye's flat. Dejia pitched the driver a couple of cyber-quid. "Thanks," Dejia said to him.

Mye lived on the outskirts of Kyuss Valley. She was a spoiled little thing too growing up; Dejia hated this about her when they'd first met. But, after the two of them had turned a few tricks together back in the day- Dejia saw Mye for who she really was. And, aside from sort-of being business partners for a little while, the two of them had history. Mye and Dejia used to date; before the war, before the degradation of Kyuss Valley, before Ducati, before Mariam.

Dejia hated that bitch, Mariam. She'd stolen Mye from her after the three of them had all slept together.

Dejia always believed that sex and relationships were two different things. In that outside of a relationship- sex was just sex. Inside of a relationship- sex was love disguised as lust. But, when the two of them came together… it didn't always mix. In fact, Dejia even sometimes vomited at the thought and taste of Mariam, still. She left a sour taste in her mouth; one that Dejia would never forget.

"Hey, girl." Mye said to Dejia as she opened the door.

Mye was wearing a short black robe. Her mechanics dangled from without her fleece cover-up. Dejia ignored them, unintentionally.

"Hey, girl." Dejia said.

"What brings you around here? Haven't seen your pretty face in a while," Mye asked.

"I guess they're after me again. Two of em' popped in and tried to pay me a little visit…" Dejia said.

"Yeah, so I've heard. Everything okay, love?" Mye asked, fixing her mechanical breasts up inside of her robe. Her vaginal port glowing; a hollow blue light shone from beneath the crotch of her robe. She still had feelings for Dejia. And, vice-versa really. She wanted Dejia to see how she had blossomed in the past few years. Her tits were up almost a whole two cup sizes, thanks to Mariam.

"Yeah, just tired. I need a place to crash," Dejia said.

"Well, come on in," Mye replied, seductively.

"Thanks, Mye. Only for a few days, until I figure this out."

"What are you going to do?" Mye asked.

"I don't know. I want to kill… all of them."

"All of who?"

"Ducati, those fucking Anodes, Mariam. Every last fucking one of them," Dejia said as she pulled out her gun from her messenger bag and cleaned it with the bottom Mye's robe.

This started to turn Mye on, producing a slight spark, a shallow hint of blue flickered again from beneath her robe.

"Mmm, You know me, I like it when a girl gets fucking nasty. C'mon now, put that thing down and let's talk…" Mye said to her.

Dejia put her gun down on the coffee table as Mye sat back on the couch provocatively, exposing part of her vaginal port. Dejia couldn't help but notice; she peeked at it a few times as it glowed. Mye was trying to beckon her. Dejia reminisced in her mind the way that vaginal port had felt wrapped around her fingertips. She could still feel it like it was yesterday. Although, the thought of it was distantly numb. She missed the depths of Mye's inner glow- her spinning mechanics of fuck and pleasure; of lust and also beauty.

Dejia started to emotionally crave Mye.

Mye's seduction tactics appeared to be working.

Dejia felt sick and confused.

Dejia peeked at Mye's vaginal port again, this time she could see a little bit of her liquids leaking out of it. Mye was getting wet. Dejia fixed herself and rubbed *her* vaginal port a bit at the same time, hiding what she was really doing from Mye. But, Dejia, she didn't feel a thing when she touched herself. She felt cavernous and hollow. She felt nothing.

Something inside her was missing.

Jon R. Meyers is an author at Riot Forge *and* Dynatox Ministries *based out of East Borneo, New Jersey. His work has appeared in a number of various publications in Cult, Horror, and Weird Fiction realms. Jon is twenty-nine years old and is currently residing in the murky depths of Northwest Indiana.*

For more information please feel free to visit him at amazon.com/author/jonrmeyers or jonrmeyers.wordpress.com

THE I.S. MAN COMETH
by David S. Wills

"I'm not like other girls."

No, of course you're not, he thought. You're all fucking unique.

"I don't like the stuff they like, y'know?"

No, of course you don't. You're different. You're the special one.

She was looking at him like she expected him to reply, so he did: "Well, what do you like?"

"I'm not into like vampires or any of that shit. I'm not one of those Twilight girls. That's teen bullshit."

Well, that's a relief. How many women had asked him to bite their necks while he fucked them, or worse... call them Bella?

"So then, tell me: What exactly is it that turns you on? And please don't say Fifty Shades of Fucking Grey."

She snorted. "No! Do I look like some bored housewife?"

Yes, that's exactly what you look like. Some bored housewife who married too early, got bored, and tells her dumbfuck husband that she's out at yoga with Carol when in fact she's soliciting male prostitutes and taking them to the cheapest motel in town.

"No, sweetie, that's not what you look like. You're a princess."

She smiled and sipped cheap white wine. "No, I'm not. I'm bad."

Here it was. The moment of truth. Everyone had something they didn't want to ask their husband, or couldn't ask him. Something they thought was dark or special, but which was in fact perfectly banal. Besides, their husband was probably sitting at home right now, jacking it to something far more depraved.

She licked her lips and sipped a little more of the awful white wine.

"Go on then, tell me," he said. Then, deciding it was time to play the role a little, he added: "Stop teasing me, baby. Tell me what you want me to do to you."

"I like your type," she said.

"And what's that? Tall, dark, handsome?"

"Yeah. And foreign."

"I'm from Pasadena…"

"You look, like, Iranian or something…"

"I'm American."

She punched him playfully on the arm. "You can't fool me, Mr. Bad Guy. You're a sleeper agent, isn't that right? You were planted here in America by I.S.I.S to behead naughty American girls. That's my type of man. The take-no-prisoners type."

"What does I.S.I.S stand for?" he asked.

"You tell me. You're the terrorist. The big, sexy terrorist."

"They usually say, 'I.S.' It stands for 'Islamic State.'"

"Well, you'd know! They planted you here years ago for the invasion of America. When I saw you I just knew it. So now I'm on to you, what're you going to do about it, huh? You gonna blindfold me? You gonna tie me up? You gonna whip me? I just know you're gonna behead me." She bit her lip hard. "Oh yeah," she moaned. "You're gonna saw my head right off."

They're all Fifty Shades of Fucking Grey girls whether they know it or not.

"Come on, Bad Guy. Come up, Mr. I.S.I.S… I mean *I.S. Man.* Punish me! I'm a naughty American girl."

He stood up and towered over her as she sat on the edge of the bed, grinning stupidly and staring up at his dark eyes.

"I want you to lie face down on the bed, while I go to my car and get some tools for the job. I have a camera, some rope, a blindfold, and my… big sword."

She giggled and rolled over onto the bed, a flash of polka dot panties as her skirt rode up.

The man walked over to the door, opened it, and headed to his car. On the way he pulled out his cell phone and dialed a number.

"We're on," he said. "You won't believe how easy this one is going to be."

David S. Wills *is the author of* The Dog Farm, Scientologist! William S. Burroughs and the 'Weird Cult', *and* Six Stories. *He is also the founding editor of* Beatdom *and* Fuck Fiction. *He earned his MA in American Literature in Scotland, trained as a farmer in California, spent most of his adulthood teaching kindergarten in South Korea, owned an Irish bar in Cambodia, and now works as a professor of academic writing in China.*

I FUCKED
SLENDER MAN
by Emma Steele

Virginia's panties were wet as she roamed the halls of Killmeister High, passing gorgeous guys with six pack abs as they carried their textbooks in front of them.

She didn't know this, but the reasons why the guys were carrying textbooks was to hide their erections, which popped up every time they stole a look at Virginia. She was stunning: long blonde hair down to her heart-shaped ass, voluptuous lips, green eyes, and great double D-sized tits. But she had no idea of how pretty she was. She thought no one wanted to touch her, to give her the love that she craved, to fulfill her human urges and desires.

If only the guys weren't so intimidated by her beauty. No one ever talked to her, and she thought this was because something was wrong with her. But she didn't have any girlfriends because they were all jealous of her. As for the guys, they considered her the hottest girl in school. She was more mature-looking than the other girls, and could have passed for a 22-year-old. Whenever the guys had sex with her classmates, they would close their eyes and pretend they were pounding away at Virginia.

Virginia got to her classroom and walked inside, but the guys kept their textbooks pressed up against their crotches. They didn't want their unsightly, large bulges to embarrass them in front of the girls they had sex with. They feared losing their opportunities for sex considering it would have been more difficult to fuel their sexual fantasies if they were being intimate with their hands rather than other girls.

Virginia sat at her desk and the bell rang, signaling the beginning of seventh period. Mr. Franklin began his lecture about the Inca Empire. Ordinarily, talk of human sacrifice would have interested

Virginia, but the drone of her teacher's voice caused her eyelids to get heavy. She put her head on her desk and dreamt of meeting Brad Wilkes underneath the bleachers during a football game.

Brad stared into Virginia's eyes with intense lust.

Brad must really like me if he blows off the big game to be with me, she thought as she removed his belt with her teeth.

The crowd cheered and she stripped Brad of his jeans, anxious to discover what awaited her underneath his tight boxer briefs. She licked her lips and unwrapped her present.

Brad stiffened to a full ten inches.

Virginia teased him by slowly licking the head of his penis. When she sensed he couldn't take it anymore, she deep-throated it and continued jerking her head up and down until the quarterback moaned in pleasure.

As she persisted with the oral pleasure, she felt a tickle in her throat. The tickle changed into a wave of pain.

She stopped the blowjob and stared down at Brad's lap.

His penis was now fifty feet long and it had grown so high that it had passed through the bleachers.

"What's wrong, baby?" Brad asked. "Keep going! I was about to cum."

Virginia looked back at him. Murderous eyes glowed red.

She woke up to her classmates' laughter, then she realized she was screaming. Despite her terror, she realized her sex dream had awoken something inside her. Brad's monstrous penis may have frightened her, but there was something about it that she liked.

No, there was something that she loved.

And it scared her.

--o0O0o--

That night, she stood staring out the window, thinking about her dream as she stroked her thigh. She noticed cars parked in the distance, across the street from her house. That meant the kids in her class were out tonight in the woods, probably drinking beer around a fire. *Why should they get to have all the fun?* she thought.

She opened her door, slowly and carefully, so her parents wouldn't hear it creak, tiptoed down the stairs, and crept out through the front door.

Walking through the woods, she heard moaning.

As she got closer, she saw her classmates in the light of a campfire, having an orgy.

Embarrassed, she stayed hidden and watched. It excited her to see all the boys who she had crushes on having sex, even if seeing Brad thrusting into Nancy Kensington made her insanely jealous. She wished Brad, or any of the boys for that matter, had asked her to meet him in the woods tonight, but watching from afar would have to do. Little did she know, but those boys who she was keeping on an eye on as she thrust her hands up inside herself were imagining their partners were Virginia.

Hours later, everyone, including Virginia, ejaculated at the exact same moment. Then everyone, except Virginia, passed out on the ground. She remained wide awake. Feeling an urge to get a closer look at her classmates as they slept, she left her hiding place and approached.

She watched Brad Wilkes snoring beside Nancy. She was such a snob! Why did she get to be with Brad?

He looked so cute while he slept. Maybe it was kind of creepy to watch him like this, but she didn't care. It's not like she would get another chance.

Brad's face started to vibrate as she stared into what would have been his deep blue eyes if he had happened to be awake.

She looked at the palms of her hands. Her skin was also vibrating and her blood vessels bulged in and out with every half second. A high-pitched squeal attacked her eardrums and she clutched her ears and collapsed.

A thin, yet immense shadow fall over her body. She turned around to discover the shadow's source and saw a dark man in the distance. He was impossibly slender and impossibly tall. She couldn't tell the difference between his arms and the tree branches that were behind him. He wore a dark suit and a black tie.

Am I dreaming? she wondered.

The man approached. His movement resembled that of a daddy longlegs. Virginia could now distinguish his arms from the tree branches. Each of his fingers extended out by what could have been ten feet. There was no way the hands belonged to a human.

The long fingers caressed Virginia, rubbing up and down her body.

Virginia gasped in pleasure. It had been so long since she had known the touch of another.

She looked at the man and started feeling lightheaded. It was as if his face was entirely blank. She knew she should have been frightened of a face that lacked eyes, a nose, and a mouth, but something about it comforted her. It seemed kind. Handsome even in a strange way that she couldn't comprehend. She imagined resting in her lap, moving itself rhythmically until it brought her to ecstasy.

The man's fingers moved over Virginia's bikini line and stopped.

Blood spurted out of her nose, followed by a headache, nausea, and exhaustion.

And a loss of consciousness.

--oOOo--

Virginia woke up the next morning in her bed, with little memory of what had occurred the night before. All she remembered was something about the woods and long fingers. There was a trace of something left behind…fulfillment. For as long as she could remember, she had felt as if a piece of her were missing, and now this feeling had gone away.

She got out of bed, felt dizzy, and collapsed back onto it. Then she threw up onto the floor.

"Mom!" she yelled. "I feel sick. Don't think I can go to school today."

Her mother came into the room, saw the vomit, and headed out to the bathroom to get a thermometer to check Virginia's temperature.

"Can you get the thermometer that goes in my butt?" Virginia asked.

The mother turned. "No, I can certainly not. You haven't used it since kindergarten. What has gotten into you, Ginny?"

"*Please*, Mom," she pleaded.

"I'm sorry, no." She patted Virginia on the head. "I'll be right back with the big girl's thermometer."

Before Virginia knew it, her mother was back.

She put the thermometer into her daughter's mouth, left it there for a few minutes, and took it out. "101 degrees," she said. "Someone is staying home from school today." She pulled the covers over Virginia. "I'll take you to do the doctor tomorrow if your fever doesn't go down. Now lie back and relax. I'm going to get you some water."

Virginia closed her eyes and fell asleep. It did not take long to dream. She found herself in a house that was different from her own. There was something about the walls. She rubbed her hands against them. They felt flesh-y. She leaned in for a closer inspection.

They were made of children!

The corpses of children had been stitched together to create this horrible house.

Virginia gagged at the smell of rot. One of the corpses said, "Hello, Mommy."

The children opened their eyes. They were no longer rotting. No longer were they corpses. Besides being sewn together to create walls—and a roof—they were perfectly normal children. They didn't seem upset about being part of a wall. Two girls were even playing patty-cake.

"What are you doing here?" Virginia asked the children.

The walls throbbed. "The Slender Man! The Slender Man is coming!" the children said.

The strange man from the woods approached and Virginia felt something she had never experienced before: love. She looked at the man, confused about why she was feeling this way. Never had she felt so passionately toward another human being.

But nothing about the man appeared to be human.

He curved the shape of his head into a grin, causing Virginia to feel a sense of peace.

Then what had appeared to be the waist of his pants stretched into the shape of a penis.

Virginia stared at it in now. It was long, luscious, and as thick as a two-liter bottle of RC Cola. She wanted it inside her now.

The man's penis extended itself to a total of—oh my god!— twenty five feet. It formed the shape of a hand, lifted up Virginia's nightgown, and entered her sex.

"The children shall be taken by the dark!" she moaned, perplexed about the meaning of the words that were leaving her mouth. "And the unjust—*oh!*—the unjust will no longer be deprived entrance through the gates of heaven."

The dark man's erection lifted Virginia to the roof. Roof children giggled at her. She closed her eyes, wishing to be alone in her revelry. The man thrust himself in and out of her. It was as if his penis was running itself through the entirety of Virginia's body.

Virginia choked. She choked again. The man's penis hit the tip of her esophagus.

Yes, he penis *was* passing through her body.

She continued to choke, but realized it wasn't an unpleasant sensation like it was in the real world. Instead, it felt fantastic. As if she had a G-Spot in her throat and the man was hitting it at just the right angle. He also happened to be hitting her actual G-Spot. Not too hard, not too soft, but just right. "Oh god! Oh god! Oh god!" she yelled.

The man's legs grew, raising him to the ceiling. "There are no gods in my domain," he said, then kissed her tenderly on the neck with his face-grin. He thrust into her, deeper and deeper, and his penis emerged out of her mouth as if her body were a jack-in-the-box.

Virginia stroked her dark lover and his wet cock was the texture of velvet. It slid in and out of her mouth. She thought about the girls in school bragging to their friends about the sexual acts they had performed on their boyfriends the night before. She couldn't wait to tell someone about having sex and giving a blowjob and a handjob *at the exact same time*. But wait…what was she thinking? None of this was real.

Or was it? she wondered as she woke up in her bedroom, still tasting the sweet flavor of her dark lover's secretions.

--oO0o--

The next day, Virginia was feeling better, so she returned to school. The hallways seemed emptier than usual. She wondered if no one had bothered to tell her that it was Senior Cut Day. But didn't that happen near the end of the semester rather than the middle? It was strange. She hadn't yet seen any of the football team, nor their girlfriends. *They probably just didn't tell me where they were going,* Virginia thought as she walked into her Spanish class. *Why do I have to be so unpopular.*

She took her seat and the bell rang. She turned around to look for Brad Wilkes, who was in this class and usually sat in the back, but his seat was empty.

"Attention, students," the school principal said over the loudspeaker. "Today is a sad day at Killmeister High. A number of our students have been missing since Wednesday night, including Brad Wilkes and the rest of the football team—"

Where could Brad be? Virginia wondered. She hoped he was okay.

"If anyone has any information pertaining to their whereabouts," the principal said, "please come to my office immediately."

Wasn't he there that night in the woods? She wished she could remember what happened. Probably nothing. Her life was always filled with absolutely nothing. Things of significance only occurred in her dreams. Yes, Brad had been in the woods, but she was only dreaming.

"Our prayers are with the students and their families."

--oO0o--

Virginia couldn't stop asking herself, "But what if it wasn't a dream?" She kept thinking it over and over again as she tried to fall asleep. Before she knew it, the clock hit 3 A.M.

Tired of not being able to sleep, she decided to investigate her doubts by going into the woods and didn't even bother to change out of her pajamas.

She walked for a few minutes until reaching a clearing. Toward the center of it were the remnants of a campfire. Upon reaching the fire pit, she saw something out of the corner of her eye that caught her attention. She looked down and saw a Killmeister Appleknocker's football jacket.

She picked it up and traced her finger over the name sewn into the back of the jacket: "Wilkes."

She panicked and dropped the jacket, feeling like she was in danger.

She tried to run, but her legs were frozen in place.

Maybe Brad and his friends were just playing hooky. Yeah, that was probably it. She had nothing to fear. Nothing. But why couldn't she move? She reached down and grabbed one of her feet, but it was as if it were nailed to the ground.

Then the man from here dreams appeared out from the shadows.

Her dream was true! Her dream was true! She was suddenly frightened for Brad, for his safety.

But wait—she couldn't care less. Brad was completely insignificant to her. What was happening? He had always been so important to her. Since she first saw him in kindergarten, not a day had passed when he wasn't in her thoughts.

Virginia turned toward the dark man and felt the same love she had felt in her dream, something she had never experienced when it came to Brad. How could she feel this way toward such a strange creature? It was almost as if it were love at first sight, but that only happened in the movies. If it ever actually ever happened in real life, and it probably didn't, the guy would have to be really gorgeous. Why else would someone feel an overwhelming passion toward someone who they didn't know?

The slender man's twelve-foot frame dwindled down to Virginia's height—as if he were kneeling—and he held out his hand toward her.

She reached for it without a second thought, and it felt fish-like. *What a gentleman,* she thought. Why couldn't boys her own age, her own species, treat her as kindly as her darling? But what was his name? "Who are you?" she asked.

The man held his long index finger to his lips, shushing her, then he lead her further into the woods.

A few minutes into their romantic moonlit stroll and they came across an area of land where bursts of flame sprouted out of the ground in the shape of toadstool. They progressed further, and Virginia saw a cabin in the distance. There was something peculiar about it, but they were too far away for Virginia to know why. It was as if the cabin wasn't made of wood. Instead, its texture shimmered like the stars. "Where are you taking me?" she asked.

This time, the man put his finger to her lips. She ran her tongue over it. Her passion felt electric. She wrapped her lips around it and jerked her head, moving it up and down her throat, hoping to give the man pleasure, a teaser for what was to come.

The man moaned, letting out a sound that was the equivalence of one thousand simultaneous car crashes.

Virginia was ready to tear off the man's clothes. She wasn't sure if it was possible. They seemed as if they were fused to his body. Regardless, she didn't think it would have been appropriate. What if somebody saw them? It would be inappropriate. She needed to calm her sexual appetite and wait until they were out of sight, like inside that peculiar cabin that was ahead. But she was being silly. There was no one around to see them in the middle of the woods in the middle of the night.

Virginia wrapped her hand around the man's crotch. "Can we?"

The word, HALT, attacked her mind like a fist to the face.

She yanked her head back, removing his finger from her mouth, then she took her hand back with a loud humph. Massaging the pain in her head, she still allowed the man to lead them toward the cabin.

"Ow, ow, ow," she repeated with each step.

The slender man turned around and his tie lifted up by itself, wound itself around her neck, choking her.

She gasped for breath, but it was over in an instant—the tie unwrapped itself and traveled back to the man's shirt, taking with it all of her pain.

Then they were in front of the cabin, and Virginia discovered why it had seem peculiar: it was made from the bodies of squirming children. It was the house from her dream. "How can it be made from children?" she asked.

Ignoring her, the man led her through the children arranged in the shape of a front door, through a hallway, and into a bedroom. Virginia's missing classmates were in a pile on the floor, tumbling against each other in a sexual frenzy. On top of the pile was a blanket and pillows, making it seem as if it were intended for sleeping.

The slender man lay on the bed and indicated that Virginia should join him by patting the top of Nancy Kensington's head as she licked Brad's shaft. Virginia obeyed, discovering that lying on the bodies of writhing teenagers was a lot more comfortable than she had expected.

The man leaned toward her, and out of an invisible mouth, spat out a liquid onto Virginia's chest.

The liquid scurried up and down her pajamas and ate through them as they sizzled and smoked. Within seconds, she found herself naked.

The man traced his long fingers over Virginia's flat stomach and up to her fantastic set of breasts. Virginia purred as they tweaked her nipples, watching Brad's face twist into a state of ecstasy. She felt no jealousy. She was glad Brad was safe and enjoying himself. It didn't matter that he and Nancy were together. The slender man was the man who Virginia was supposed to be with. She knew this was true in her heart.

The dark man sat up and grew in stature. She watched in amazement as he rose toward the roof. It looked as if he wasn't slowing down. When he was about to crash into it, the children accommodated him by crawling on top of each other, higher and higher and higher. *Won't he ever finish?* Virginia asked herself. It seemed as if his ascent would go on forever.

And then it stopped.

Virginia stared up at his blank face, licking her lips and wondering how she could somehow who lacked features so handsome.

She reached behind the man to feel his tight ass, but discovered that he didn't have one! It was like touching a wooden board with a rubbery texture.

Virginia's mind was invaded by the word, STOP.

She moved her hand back. The man flipped is body over in one slither.

Buttocks sprouted out of the back of him, the most beautiful ass she had ever seen. Within her heart she knew it was the most beautiful ass that had ever been possessed since the dawn of mankind. She grabbed its cheeks, savoring its exquisite beauty and texture.

STOP

Frustrated, she obeyed.

Then his butt grew until perhaps it was the biggest butt that a guy had ever had, pushing Virginia off the bed of flesh and forcing her against the wall. Despite the butt's immense girth, Virginia wasn't disgusted. Rather, she was even more turned on. And the butt didn't stop there. It got bigger and bigger until it engulfed her.

Virginia suddenly found herself inside her lover's anus. She had expected to face many difficulties throughout her life, but this was one she had never anticipated. Nevertheless, the inside of his anus wasn't gross or anything, which really surprised her. Instead, it smelled like cologne. Obsession for Men, she thought.

Then she felt hands wrap themselves around her body. Unnaturally long fingers vibrated over her skin, causing her to moan. She was euphoric, as if her entire body were a giant clitoris. Slowly, the hands thrust her up. She screamed in pleasure as she journeyed up through his digestive system, through the twists and turns of his intestines, and through his stomach

Wait…were those penguins?

Yes, they were penguins. Why were live penguins roaming around her man's stomach?

Why cares? Virginia had never felt so much pleasure in her life. It was almost too much for her to handle. But not nearly there. Almost there. Almost. Almost. She could take it. Who cares about the penguins? Who cares?

Penguins. Penguins. Penguins. Penguins. Pen…guins. Penguin. Penguin. Penguin. Pen…guin. *Penguin penguin penguin penguin penguins!*

She was carried up through his throat and out of his mouth—where the air was fresher and easier to gasp into—then back down into his anus.

She went up and down, up and down, her skin rubbing against his insides, the friction driving the lovers wild. Virginia heard the slender man screaming in sexual bliss from outside himself. It sounded like the neighing of a demonic horse. Knowing she was fulfilling her man's manly needs and desires increased the intensity of pleasure.

He lifted her through him, faster and faster and faster.

And she. And she. And she. It was too much. Too much. She never wanted it to end. But she couldn't. She couldn't go on like this. It was impossible. So impossible. It had to end. She couldn't take it. Couldn't take

And then she burst into fire.

Emma Steele *is the author of the* Fuck All Monsters *series, which includes* Debbie Does Monsterland *and* Alien vs. Debbie.

THE TIME I LET AN OLDER MAN FONDLE MY PENIS
by Joseph Wargo

Happy Prostitution Day!

Romance is once again forced upon us on this, the day when it is socially acceptable to accept flowers and chocolates in return for anal sex and blow jobs. Allow me then this reflection on a traveling tale of lust.

There are three things that happen when you travel. One thing is a story where nothing happens. Another thing is that you make something happen to have a story. The third thing was a story before it happened, a story waiting to happen. I travel a lot and have experienced these three things. This story is all of them.

This is a story about curiosity.

It's August in Houston, Texas. Fuck. It's fucking hot. 100+ degrees. And no clouds. I'm hitchhiking, standing on a westbound onramp for Interstate 10. It's a shitty onramp. There is little room for cars to safely pull over, but I'm too tired to find a better ramp and delirious enough not to care.

The night before, I had Greyhounded from New Orleans. Only paying to go to Baton Rouge, but stowing away to the end of the line. I spent most of the night sitting in the station waiting for sunrise. A cop outside the station told me not to wander the streets or I'd get attacked and they'd take my pack. I listened to him. Sort of.

Inside the station this guy got my attention. He saw me using my laptop and asked me if I'd sell it for $300. I said I would. He asked me if I was hungry and offered to buy me breakfast. The cop had told me no restaurants or diners were open and that should have been my first clue, but I was curious.

I think his name was either Andrew or Anthony. We walked down a main street into the heart of downtown. He stopped at a corner and told me he had to go hit an ATM to grab cash for the computer and I should wait for him there.

I didn't. I walked across the street, hid behind a column of some office building, and waited. Like a terrible movie, I disliked the set up and hook but wanted to see how it ended.

Time passed and I'm thinking this guy saw that I left and took off himself so I'll never know his true intentions. I waited until I noticed two different guys walking up the street from the direction I had walked with Anthony/Andrew. A gunshot went off and they started running. I decided to go too, down another street and back to the bus station.

Anywho, I digress. This is a sexy story about being manhandled by the elderly, not about how shitty Houston is.

A Porsche pulls over. Angry honks from the cars passing him to get on the freeway. I hop in. His name is Max, he's sixty-three years old and retired. He picks me up because of the heat, he can't stand to see me suffer out there. Pity rides happen and I take them all the same.

Max cranks the AC, says he can get me out of the heat for a while and serve me some lunch. I can even get a shower. Yes, yes, and yes.

We go to a house he calls his friend's house. He's housesitting for the friend. He's lying.

He fixes me up with some grub which I eat quickly. He tells me the shower is upstairs. I use it. I wash the sweat off knowing when I step back outside I will again be covered in sweat. When I exit the bathroom he shows me a guest bedroom I can take a nap in. I'm tired, and sleeping in a bed sounds glorious. I nap.

I sleep for about half an hour when I hear a knock at the bedroom door. It's Max. He's trying to get up the courage to ask me something, I can tell. He's very nervous and cute about it. He reminds me of a more attractive John McCain.

He's subtle in a not so subtle way. "Would you like to watch some porn?"

I decline. Despite my inclinations toward sexual deviancy, I'm not a overly libidinous person.

Max spills it. We're at his life partner's house who really is out of town. He claims they've been going through a rough patch and that he can no longer get an erection with him.

He asks me if he can give me a handjob. This is where curiosity takes over again. I hadn't had much experience with men up to that point, and Max seemed harmless. Earlier that month in Florida, a man had taken me to a motel and tried to have sex with me, but I deflected his advances. That guy did not ask, he just expected.

I say yes.

He takes out a bottle of lotion and I take off my pants. He rubs the lotion all over my penis and testicles until I'm hard. He then undoes his fly and begins stroking his own penis as he fondles mine. He comes fast and hard.

He asks me if I want a blowjob. I decline. This isn't about me.

We hop back in the car and he buys me some fast food for dinner, hands me ten dollars and a sack of marihuana, and drops me outside the city limits.

I am on another onramp, it's late afternoon. I think about what just occurred and realize, for the first time in my life, that I am a prostitute.

I stick my thumb out and laugh at the passing motorists.

J.W. Wargo has sex some but not all of the time. He is the author of Avoiding Mortimer. When he isn't traveling he lives at a social anarchist commune farm in Tennessee. "The Time I Let An Older Man Fondle My Penis" is reprinted from the online blog previously posted February 15th, 2013

THE PARTNERS
by Chris Meekings

The priest climbed the stairs as the rain began to fall. In one hand he carried the flint knife, which dripped crimson blood onto the stones, splashing onto the cold hard rock like lost tears. Over his shoulder was a bag made from the skin of a monkey, the black sightless, sockets of its face still staring out at the world. The priest leaned heavily on the staff clutched in his other hand, supporting nearly his full weight on the thumb thick wood. Around the wood of the staff was the figure of an entwined serpent made from metal. Its hooded head was rampant at the top of the staff, its tail pointed at the tip.

The last remnants of light played across the priest's old and cracked face, caressing his leathery skin as a lover saying farewell. The fur pelt slung over his shoulder, a trophy from his youth, kept out the worst of the wind. He grunted as he took the next step, exhaling deeply and drawing in strength on his in breath.

The stairs were deep and worn with age, bending in the middle as if a savage weight had been placed upon them. Hacked from limestone by master craftsmen the blocks were light grey, dusted with black flecks. They made a dry rasping sound under the priest's sandals as he climbed, he did not hear the noise. His whole world was reduced to the next step, and then the next step, and so on, up and up, to the summit.

Birds cawed in the trees surrounding the temple, but he did not hear their sounds. Wind whipped at his feathered headdress, but it made no impression on him. His bones ached with weariness and rivulets blood ran from cuts along his arms and torso, but it was nothing to him. His nose picked up the fetid, hot smell of animals, birds, plants and decay in the jungle around him, but he ignored them. Sweat dripped from his body as the sticky, humid air clasped around him, he simply endured the discomfort. His focus was on the next step, like a beam of pure light breaking through clouds. His heart beat, his breath went in and out, and he took then next step in his stride.

He reached the top of the temple, in his time, and stood, feet planted on the ground, belly defiant, chest pulled up and head erect. The blood fell from his stone knife making a pool of scarlet at his feet. Firmly planting his staff next to him, he rooted it in a metal disc set into the stonework.

"I have come," he said, his deep voice filling the top of the temple. The wind moved around him and the clouds formed over him, but the world did not stir.

"I have come," he repeated, with deeper resonance.

"So you have," said the wind.

"Show yourself."

"I shall not."

"Blood for the bloodqueen," he said and pulled a human heart from his shoulder bag. He threw it at the ground in front of himself. It hit the stone wetly, coagulating black blood, seeped from its depths.

"What is that?" asked the wind.

"You know what that is. We have danced this dance before."

"Yet the dance must be completed. What is that?"

"My competitor," said the priest. "Two go for communion, only one gets to the top. You know this: blood for the bloodqueen. Here is blood, show yourself. Show yourself, Golga."

"Very well," said the wind.

She sparkled out of the air in front of the priest. Her hair was long and black as midnight. Her face was slender and elfin. She wore no clothes, her hips were full, her breasts ripe and her waist slim and graceful. Firelight burnt in her yellow eyes, reflecting a hundred sacred dances completed around a hundred bonfires. She was woman, she was the storm, she was the bloodqueen, she was Golga, she was manifest.

"What is it you want?" she asked, a half smile creeping across her face.

"Communion: I wish to ride the lightning."

"You wish to ride the lightning?" she asked. Her smile grew wider as a perfect eyebrow arched up in question.

"I need to ride the lightning."

"Need?"

"I must ride the lightning. The storms must come. The rain must fall."

"The storms will come in time. The rain will fall in time," said Golga, turning away.

"They must come now," the priest insisted.

Golga spun to face him. The fire in her eyes was raging like a burning village. Her hair reared out from her head like snakes poised to strike.

"You do not command me," she hissed.

"I must ride the lightning," the priest insisted. His face was set hard as stone, his eyes were full and present.

Her hair flattened against her head, and her eyes became two burning coals.

"Sacrifice?" she asked.

The priest looked startled for a moment. His knife pointed at the heart at her feet.

"Blood for the bloodqueen," he said.

"He was not worthy. He was inferior. You came up here. Sacrifice," she purred the last word like a pleased cat.

The priest stared at her for a moment. Then he said, "Blood for the bloodqueen."

He took his stone knife in his right hand and held his left arm out straight. The knife pieced his bicep just below the knot of his shoulder. Deep, rich blood welled up as he dragged the gash to his elbow.

Golga smiled and clasped her hands together.

"Old fool," she laughed at him, "you wish to ride the lightning, to see the storm, to stare at life itself? Your heart will cave in and I will eat it. Your blood will boil and I will drink it. Your soul will scream and I will laugh."

"Enough teasing, bitch," snarled the priest. "Cast your storm. I have come here, as you planned. I have killed my competitor, as you required. I have cut myself, as you wished. Kill me, if you can."

"Die then, you old fuck," she said and unleashed the storm.

Boiling clouds overhead burst like rotten fruit. Thick rain slashed down at the priest. He drank what he could and spat it back in her face. Howling winds rasped at his skin. They tore the fur pelt from his body and he still stood defiant, naked and erect. Hale tore from the sky, pelting his skin, causing gashes and bruises to flow with his blood. He dodged what he could and jested at the rest of his wounds. Lightning flew from the sky in arcing cracks. The priest caught it on the snake head of his staff and conducted it down into the temple.

Then Golga manifested again. She came as a flurry straight for his naked form. Biting him, hitting him, kissing him, loving him, crucifying him, enveloping him, throwing him away. She tore at him, she healed him, she punched him, she caressed him, she screamed at him, she sucked him, she unleashed him, she set him free. She was in him, around him, above him, below him, together with him, apart from him.

He was in her, thrusting, pushing, snarling, biting back, pinning her beneath him, holding on to her, trying to stay in the moment, fucking her, being her, tearing at her, loving her. He was always on the edge of collapse, of retreat, but staying present by his own sheer will power. Their sweat mingled together as their bodies writhed, sliding slickly across each other. They pulled and thrust together - bit and laughed together, clinging onto each other in the eye of the storm.

He took what he could. He held her in his gaze as long as he could. He loved her as long as he could. He hated her as much as he could. He was with her for an eternity, but it would not be enough.

When they had finished, the priest still remained, drained but alive. He panted deeply, his chest heaving.

"You dance a good dance," she smiled at him. He smiled back and she disappeared into infinity.

He knew that it had only been a part of the storm with which he had danced. The tiniest fraction, of her smallest finger and it was more power than he could take. She had been kind to him.

His back hurt. His arm throbbed from his wound. The sounds of the jungle birds were music to his ears. The sweat was all over him in a thick sheen. The biting insects would soon find him. The rain had come and the jungle could rejuvenate. The village would need him soon. There were always obligations but, for now, he could rest in the moment. He was calm, at peace. The little death had occurred.

"I love you," said the wind.

The priest laughed and opened his heart.

"I love you too," he said.

Chris Meekings lives in the city of Gloucester in the UK, if you'd ever been to Gloucester you'd understand why he sits inside and makes things up.

His work has recently appeared on Bizarro Central's Flash Fiction Friday. His bizarro novella Elephant Vice was recently released as part of the New Bizarro Authors Series.

by William Burroughs II
and Gerard Malanga

Now the judgement of things to come—let's all tell where we are from and why—Oh Kiki the way things fit together shell asshole sunrise—vegetable passions caught your heart—what is difficult is crossed out—In the boat house we committed the action of sodomy. Now I am coming in and out of you in dreams of corduroy but who recovers from the weight of the tornado fiend? dream of the dashboard his name is John. Aristo Hotel who am I flower blooming from the well—the laundromat went round and round—dying in furnished rooms—ah bin called so many names and such I couldn't begin to put it all down on this sheet ha ha au revoir—my cock's hard egg—nog in Cambridge—Orphan Annie's hold out 15-23— whistling down a dark alley with a straw cock and a thin chest (what is difficult is crossed out) vaguely in flesh memories blurred to wraiths of wind—in my boots in my blue wool shirt—huge boulders in the dark ravine and a fish the Spanish people eat (what is difficult is crossed out) couldn't get me near one red they are— where suns shine into the broken eyes birds are singing on the back porch—scar tissue again in layers flowers sprouting out the ass— the end of world skidded into an arch the signature of all things leaking from the frayed edges of control—ach! indeed pearls and swine—then coming crowning ring the gong—cut him down— gong! gong! cut him down—Ach! Conger eels upon us—so Dallas phones the Uranians and good bye letters lie under smelly window panes bending to years ago—The Claytom St—I am over here come back if you want—the leg and the thigh—all the parts want a name what did I pay them?

Afterbirth of dream—the white cat bites my finger—old flower smell of young nights—room over the florist shop—sad stagnant

St. Louis morning outside—M.B. stands over me naked on the bed one foot in a sweat sock rubbing my crotch—'You come with me to jack off in 1920?'—not much time left—the gun in a locker—windy streets—flares—this long ago address—*flaming hand from old Westerns—a long shot with a hand gun*—broken sky—black out falling—dim voice cracked—*Know who I am?*—He is dying—I remember the route I took the day I was drafted driving through a town of red stone—an area of bearded sleazies who do quick tricks to avoid my gaze—aliens the human shell is thin—She made my bedroll all wrong and I had to do it over I will not hold a discussion in the nude—The Greeks have a reputation for sharp dealing—dressing in a picture window—outside the black St. Louis morning—'I have been ill for a day'—he couldn't get it up—'slipped in she did—those two horrors—so should I go to Wisconsin?' (article 10 below) pale blue summer sky on the back porch of his farm. John did you buy the hotel?—I went to the toilet—I was in the toilet and when I reached the boy came at me—**fire—factory that he was nowhere near—**fire—factory that he was nowhere near—open this up and break it so I can touch you* Mix with the roaring sky of broken film streets half buried of quiet deserted suburbs 'Calling Panama—you should slide into space more gracefully—A black belt you got it—Regret I have but one—quein es?—flapping streets and buildings round and round faster faster—60 tornadoes gulf states today—1884 fine works of pickled flesh—the thawed room—P.W jacked off into the sink—a young man naked *urinates with half erection a toilet with red clay on the seat where the banks are under the shadows of teenagers' bellies Know who I am?*

William Burroughs II *was an American novelist, short story writer, essayist, painter, and spoken word performer.*

Now the judgement of things
to come--lets all tell where
we are from and why--Oh Kiki
the way things fit together
shell asshole sunrise--veget-
able passions caught your XXXX
heart--what is difficult is
crossed out--In the boat house
we committed the action of
sodomy.Now I am coming in
and out of you in dreams of
corduroy but who recovers
from the weight of the tornado
fiend? dream of the dashboard
his name is John.Aristo Hotel
who am I flower blooming from
the well-- the laudromat went
round and round--dying in
furnished rooms--ah bin called
so many names and such I
could'nt begin to put it'all
down on this sheet ha ha auh
revore--my cock's hard egg-
nog in Cambridge--Orphan
Annie's hold out 15-23--
whistling down a drak alley
with a straw cock and a thin
cheet XXXX(what is difficult
is crossed out) vaguely in
flesh memories blured to
wraiths of wind--in my boots
in my blue wool shirt--huge
boulders in the dark ravine
and a fish the Spanish people
eat XXXXXXXX (what is XXXXX
difficult is crossed out)
could'nt get me near one red
they are--where suns shine
into the XXXXXXXXXXXX broken
eyes birds are singing on
the back porch--scar tissue
again in layers flowers
sprouting out the ass--the
end of world skidded into
an arch the signature of all
things leaking from the frayed
edges of control--ach! indeed
pearls and swine --then coming
crowing wing the gong--cut him
down--gong!gong! cut him down
Ach! Conger eels upon us--So
Dallas phones the Uranians and
good bye letters lie under
smelly window panes bending to
years ago--The Clayton St--
I am over here come back if
you want--the leg and the
thigh--all the parts want a
name what did I pay them?

Afterbirth of dream--the white
coat bites my finger--old flower
smell of young nights--room over
the florist shop--sad stagnant
St.Louis morning outside--M.B.
stands over me naked on the bed
one foot in a sweat sock rubbing
my crotch--'You come with me to
jack off in I920?'--not much time
left--the gun in a locker--windy
streets--flares--this long ago
address--flaming hand from old
Westerns--a long shot with a
hand gun--broken sky--black out
falling--dim voice cracked--Know
who I am?--He is dying--I remember
the route I took the day I was
drafted driving through a town
of red stone--an area of bearded
sleazies who do quick tricks to
avoid my gaze--aliens the human
shell is thin--Shemade my bedroll
all wrong and I had to do it over
I will not hold a discussion in
the nude-- The Greeks have a reputation fo sharp dealing--dressing
in a picture window-- outside the
black St.Louis morning--'I have
been ill for a day'--he could'nt
get it up--'slipped in she did--
those two horrors--so I should
go to Wisconsin? ' (article 10 below
below)pale blue summer sky on the
back porch of his farm.John did
you buy the hotel?--I wnet to the
toilet--I wans in the toilet and
when I reached the the boy came
at me--fire--factory that he was
nowhere near--fire--factory that
he was nowhere near--open this up
and break it so I can touch you
Mix with the roaring sky of XXXXXX
broken film streetshalf XXXXXXX
buried of quiet deserted suburbs
'Calling Panama-- You should slide
into space more gracefully--A
black belt yo got it--Regret I
have but one--quein es?--flapping
streets and buildings round and
round faster faster-- 60 tornados
gulf XXXXX states today--I984 fine
works of pickeled flesh-- the
thawed room--P.W jacked off into
thh sink-p a yong man naked
XXXX urinates with half erection
a toilet with red clay on the seat
where the banks are under the
shadows of teen ager's belly's
Know who I am?

by Annie Sprinkle

by Annie Sprinkle

Michael Allen Rose and Sauda Namir, 'Togetherness'

by Robert Branaman

by Robert Branaman

'Bloody' by Veronica Chaos

Nov. 23, 1963

Alone
in that same self where I always was
with Kennedy throat again bloodied in Texas
the television continuous blinding two nuder days
with Charlie muttering in his underwear strewn bedroom
with Neal running down the hall shouting about the racetrack
with Ann with her white legs and clit under the Cupid thigh
with Lucille talking to herself, feeding the pregnant cat Alice
with Anne warning her poducuxed wash & the bare nemaled chest of now later
with David's red wine fireplace casting shadows back to the darkness farmboy
      faggot of Wichita, on fire in wallstreet
with Lance with his crummy painting & leopard skin breast seeking to buy
      a motorcycle to crosscountry bulling a man
with the manuscripts of neutrition Lucelle the New York suicide on the
      round mahogony table hear the kitchen
with Carol Jones white eyeballed war-cry warned, babbling in psilocvin
      blue-sober
with myself on naked clock-fingertip't on the rented typewriter
  with Alan with horses teeth satafying demurel limiting he was intensely
      so over coffee
with Glen o'the limp & Justin the olding blackpendelen and love off in clouds
      to Mexico cactus hope
with the far lad, with bone in his ache, reading & grieving her adolescence's
      husband
with "Go to Hell" spoke on the streetcorner down Now hill in the dark of
      November night
with Judy's blood in the furnace building up veins before in the campus-forests
      in the goodlives of white-haired parents on Television
with warm Christie boy running around in railroads talking fast about his
      eyeachotds seeing true streets of '40's
with Jaime phoning collect from New York insulting him Lonesome theM
with Bonnie & sighing she was drunk & insulting on the doors, a Marks with
      a bandaged tendon hanging in front of his eyeballs
with Robert in beret & tweed beard resolutel sober no anti-dream lumpier-
      splitter rorschak universe, drinking milk,
with Jordan on the phone suave & retired joshing invisible mandalas upstairs
      from the technicolor gutter
with Larry whitehaired showing his teeth nodding in chairs week & amiable
      lost the pointlessome
with the cat curled in white fur in the kitchen chair,
with the transistor radio silent weeks on the typewriter desk,
with the novels Happiness Bastard Sheeper from Tanger Wichita and Gun
      Yesterday Today & Tomorrow
with now, with Puek age, with wild boy marking Amen poetry Over Green &
      Thieves Journal Soft Machine Genesis Reminescence Contact Kill Roy etc,
with Apparatus appearing at the doors to know white happening you wanna score
      or do I the sacred fear the saintgoof fuck the insect trust or delicious Home
with Robert in his black jacket & tie deciding to make a point of his courtesy
      over the kitchen linoleum
with the ghosts of Natalie & Peter & Krishna & Huw intoned o the hung rugs
      in the darkness of abandoned rooms
with Blue Grace in typescript stepping out of the bang on the wall, and letters
      arriving from Raleigh & Chicago
with me breaking off to remain in the other room where Adam & Eve lay
      so peti my hair aspray.

by Allen Ginsberg
& Charles Plymell

Alone
in that same self where I always was
with Kennedy throat brain bloodied in Texas
the television continuous blinking two radar days
with Charlie muttering in his underwear strewn bedroom
with Neal running down the hall shouting about the racetrack
with Ann with her white boy's ass silent under the Cupid thigh
with Lucille talking to herself, feeding the pregnant cat Alice
with Anne mourning her pockmarked womb & the hard muscled
    chest of her Lover
with David's red wine fireplace casting shadows back to the Duchess
    farmboy faggot of Wichita, on fire in main street
with Lance with his crummy painting & leopard blue breast seeking
    to buy a motorcycle to crosscountry smiling & wan
with the manuscripts of nutritious Hoselle the New York suicide on
    the round mahogany table near the kitchen
with Leroi Jones white eyeballed war-cry unread, bubbling in
    postmortem blue-sneer
with myself confused shock-fingertip't on the rented typewriter
with Alan with horse's teeth metaphysics demurely insisting he was
    intensely so over coffee
with Glen o'the lisp & Justin the olding bluejacketed man love off in
    Matoa to Mexico cactus hope
with the fat lady with babe in the auto, feeding & grieving her
    adolescent's backseat
with "Go to Hell" spoke on the streetcorner down the hill in the
    dark of November night

with Judy's blood in the furnace building up weeks before in the
    campus-forests in the bloodlines of white-haired parents on
    Television
with Christopher running around in raincoats talking fast about his
    eyesockets seeing true streets of '60's
with Jamie phoning collect from New York insulting his lonesome
    Cunt
with Nannie insisting she was drunk & insulting on the couch, &
    Marco with a bandaged tendon hanging in front of his gaptooth
with Hubert in beret & tweed beard absolutely sober on Meth-freak
    newspaper splatter Rorschach universe, drinking milk,
with Jordan on the phone suave & retired jobbing & visible mandalas
    upstairs from the technicolor gutter
with Larry whitehaired chewing his teeth nodding in chairs weak &
    amiable lost the pointlessness
with the cat curled in white fur in the kitchen chair,
with the transistor radio silent weeks on the typewriter desk,
with the novels *Happiness Bastard Sheeper from Tangier Wichita Mad*
    Cub Yesterday Today & Tomorrow
with *Now*, with *Fuck You*, with *Wild Dog Burning Bush Poetry*
    Evergreen & *Thieves' Journal Soft Machine Genesis Renaissance*
    Contact Kill Roy etc,
with spaniards appearing at the door to know what's happening you
    wanna score or am I the sacred fear for the methhead fuzz the
    insect trust or delicious Jose
with Robert in his black jacket & tie deciding to make a point of his
    courtesy over the kitchen linoleum
with the Ghosts of Natalie & Peter & Krishna & Ras intoned on the
    shag rugs in the darkness of abandoned rooms
with Blue Grace in typescript stepping out of the taxi on the wall, &
    letters arriving from Malanga & Chicago
with the breaking off to rush in to the other room where Adam &
    Eve lay to get my hair spray.

Charles Plymell is a poet, novelist, and small press publisher. Plymell has been published widely, collaborated with, and published many poets, writers, and artists, including principals of the Beat Generation.

Support the Troops By Giving Them Posthumous Boners:

Leftward-leaning Prot-priestess gets overexcited at Marine hero's funeral, causing all true red American blood to seethe

by Tom Bradley

"Behold this bleeding breast of mine
Gashed with the sacramental sign.
I stanch the blood, the wafer soaks,
High Priestess moistened death invokes.
This Bread I gorge, this Oath I swear
As I enflame myself with prayer."
    --Aleister Crowley, *Mass of the Phoenix*

Distinguished, decorated, not much longer corporeal Corporal, trenchered out piecemeal in our laps, your bronze whatzit with fig leaf clusters or almond clusters, or whatever, pinned on your thorax, reamed-out, stainless steel-stented, don't you fret, my handsome boy.

We promise not to tattle to absentee Pa that you, literally gutless, failed to complete your eighth stop-lossed tour of duty, way over there in Eye-rack, running interference for Halliburton's pricey mercenaries.

116

Not from us will ex-pregnant-teen Ma hear that you unmetaphorically crapped out before she could hold a bake sale for E-Bay body armor, your penultimate birthday-boy surprise.

Meanwhile, allow me to hoist the hem of my pastoral cassock, climb on the casket rim, and squat, knickerless, like Greer over her mirror. Pucker up, youngster. Don't pout. We intend to give you every benefit of the doubt.

Nourished from infancy on meat and sugar, you brat of an illiterate slag, reared in the roar of televised blood and shit and sperm, numbed to your neurons by the fumes of Ma's kitchenette meth lab, capable of only a bored child's-eye video-view of the manifested universe, blood addict, insane with black hate-spleen.

You popped a chubby at a pep rally back in hi-skool, got called a homo by jocks, jeered by cheerleaders. You said to yourself (back when you had tongue and lips that were something more than ash primped with jizz-colored mortuary wax), "Gol-dang, I need some o' that--what-d'-you-call-it--dissy-plin in m' life. I better enlist, yup-yup-yup."

Are you retarded enough to reckon that was an actual decision on your part? You were part of the plan all along, Corporal Corpse. Your nation was methodically over-lawyered in preparation for your nativity, divorce was facilitated, your generation well-farmed, incubated in broken homes, corn-fed golem oafs too heart- and brain-damaged to do more than rampage in a proxy war on behalf of that boa-constricting entity which I, your priestess, for self preservation's sake, even here in this Christian sanctuary, must euphemize, in a whisper, as "the Trans-national Corporatocracy."

Their pet execs in the recording industry soaked your existence, in-utero onward, with perpetual grunting decibels, drumming monotony, aural steroids. You obediently i-podded it straight into the side of your learning-disabled head while slogging through Fallujah's scab-clogged gutters.

Just following orders, carrying out YHWH's immemorial injunction from on high, as we find in today's reading from the second and third verses of the fifteenth chapter of the First Book of You-Know-Who (with wet thighs I mount the lectern, pry apart the Good Book's buttocks, and declaim):

117

"Now go and smite Amalek, and utterly destroy
all that they have, and spare them not;
but slay both man and woman, infant and suckling,
ox and sheep, camel and ass."

Such a useful runt. I brim with white phosphorous affection for you, my boy-toy. We need to breed whole fleets of Bradley Urban Assault Vehicles jam-full of lovely, drooly, bristly, backward-bending hard-ons like you.

That other military empire, Grand Assyria, whose ashes you made mud with your shit and blood, had the right idea. High on the ramparts they impaled any teen Ma, any unpatriotic hussy, who sought to procure miscarriage.

Speaking of writhing on a spike, with my sacerdotal labia majora I now squeeze your jar head. Here's a trigger for you to pull, kissy-boy. I twist your muscled neck to wring a final requiescat stiffy.

Ten-hut. Support them troops.

Tom Bradley (tombradley.org) has published twenty-five volumes of fiction, essays, screenplays and poetry with houses in the USA, Great Britain and Canada. Various of his novels have been nominated for the Editor's Book Award, the New York University Bobst Prize, and the AWP Series. 3:AM Magazine *in Paris gave him their Nonfiction Book of the Year Award in 2007 and 2009, and an excerpt from one of his latest books will appear in this year's* &Now Innovative Writing Award Anthology. *His journalism and criticism have appeared in such publications as* Salon.com, *and are featured in* Arts & Letters Daily.

Behind the White Monument
by Malcolm Laughton

Wee Johnny followed his Ma and Da down the path, past the allotments, and into the cemetery. He'd grown big enough to know a cemetery was full of people who'd gone to Heaven. They walked cinder paths under big weepy trees and marble angels; and all around gravestones stood, each every one of them taller than Johnny.

Ma and Da turned onto the long grass, full of daisies, clover, buttercups, bumblebees, and dandelions. 'The state they keep this cemetery in,' said Ma. 'It's a disgrace.' 'I've got the shears,' said Da.

They stopped at Grand Da's grave. Johnny remembered, he'd been here before. 'Well let's get to work,' said Da. 'You've got the trowel,' he said to Ma. Ma and Da had come to 'tend' the grave, Johnny remembered. He watched them work. 'Tending' was another word for 'gardening.' Johnny thought about the little garden grave – as long, as a grownup was tall. And he thought about Grand Da's skeleton, down below, and worms. He stood off the grave, but found himself standing on some other person.

Johnny got bored watching them gardening. He looked about. Gravestones stood everywhere. Rows and rows of them. Some of them taller than Ma and Da. The stones stood like silent people, all watching Johnny. He felt a little bit scared, but it was daytime, and Ma and Da were there; and the stones drew his curious eye.

One stone was different. Other stones were grey, or brown, or shiny black – but this one was shiny white. And it was big. Almost as big as a little wee house. It had columns and arches and steps – like a little wee palace for little wee people. Something to climb and play on. Johnny ran over to it, and started to climb the steps.

'Get away from there!' Da shouted at him. Johnny had done something wrong.

Johnny climbed down from the white palace. He'd hardly started to climb, before Da had stopped him. Da's voice had been angry, but Da didn't seem angry now, just telling him off, like something important Johnny didn't understand. 'Don't do that.' 'Why not?' 'Just don't! It's someone's monument.'

Johnny stood, for a very, very, very long time, watching the slow gardening. He felt eyes watching him from behind. He turned round. There was no one there, but he saw the monument. He turned back, to see his Ma and Da busy with grass and weeds. He could sneak away. If he was quiet as a mouse.

Johnny began to climb the marble steps. They were big and steep, but he climbed them. There were more steps than he thought, but then he clambered onto a flat stone slab like a table. There, in front of him, he saw a narrow place, just big enough to crawl into. He thought he saw an eye blink at him, from some magical place of apple and pear and cherry blossom. But he couldn't quite see. Unless he got closer. Johnny stuck his head in the hole. He saw a big bright room at the other end. He crawled in.

Johnny stood up, at the other end of the tunnel. The room was huge, and light pervaded the space, as if the day outside shone through translucent alabaster. Below, the light formed a haze of colour. A marble staircase descended before him. He took the steps easily, in his young adult stride. As he reached the floor of the hall, the haze of colour focused. He stood in an avenue of trees, each hanging with blossom. As he looked closer at the branches and boughs, he saw they were glass, with frozen sap in their veins; and all about, he saw the blossoms, not cherry and white, but jade and lapis lazuli. He began to walk the avenue, his head dizzy with the scent of semi-precious stone.

Johnny stopped. He noticed the absolute silence, only when it was broken. He stood and listened. It was almost not there. Audible only against the background of total quietude. A light tapping. The sound seemed to come from the wall behind the trees. He stepped between two trees, and walked the little distance to the alabaster wall.

Johnny placed his hand to the wall, feeling the smooth surface. As he moved his palm and fingers across its face, he felt tiny wrinkles, almost as if the cold surface yielded to the warm pressure. He peered in at the surface. There *were* wrinkles; and tiny cracks. He placed an ear against the alabaster. *Tick, tick, tick,* like the mating call of the death watch. He heard another sound, a faint giggle from the far end of the hall.

Johnny looked up, and caught a glimpse of a girl, her skin as pale a marble angel, her dress the colour of lapis, her eyes the colour of jade. She dashed away, through a doorway.

--o0O0o--

Johnny followed the girl's trail like a memory through a dream, along stone corridors that narrowed as he grew, moments passing years until the monument opened into outside and onto a marble path.

Johnny stepped from a white marble path, and walked onto a gloaming moor, red in the late glow of a hidden sun. In the far distance there appeared to be ancient mountains, but when he looked directly he saw a naked horizon with only one great, split shard of rock in the middle distance. A name came into his head; and he called out: *'Joan.'*

In the distance a woman in a full length, bell-shaped, blue coat turned toward him. She was slow to approach, but then quickened. When she came close enough that her big, deep, green eyes looked into his; he was not sure she was the same woman. Her face looked hostile, greedy, older. He shouted her off, and she receded into the distance, diminishing to a point, then gone. His eyes searched the horizon, and the land shimmered as if its geology was caught up in a viscous heat haze.

Walking the moor, Johnny's memory slipped and changed like the landscape. Time had no constant memory, as if some after-before dream intruded. His legs wearied under the pull of some contrary clock, its hands inconstant but galloping. He felt he was being followed. He stopped, looked round and saw low-slung, loping, scuttling figures in the middle distance. From where he stood, they looked like gangly, malformed, vermillion beetles. The oversized beetles, the size of people, seemed to back off, under his stare; but he moved on, as fast as he could without running, without stumbling.

As Johnny moved further out into the moor, he had to move slowly; the ground had become damp, like a grave for peat bog people, and the earth shifted under his tread like an unsteady membrane of rotting skin. He walked a circuitous way of steadier ground over an ever-shifting path of steppingstones. As he glanced behind, from time to time, he thought he glimpsed red specs of insects, sometimes nearer, sometimes further. For hours and days and moments, he wandered without other external reference; passing bleached and broken dead trees, and oily pools of iridescent water where sickened lurid colours mixed and swirled and whorled.

The ground hardened, and Johnny looked up.

A white crystalline desert, with jade and lapis shards, ran before Johnny. He glanced behind. The beetles had gone. Ahead of him, in the far distance, he saw a lone human figure moving. Perhaps Joan. But he could not tell from such a distance even if it was a man or a woman, or whether it was coming or going. He started in its direction, but the figure became lost in the shimmering light. Johnny trod on alone, and now he saw a loch, within a shallow glen, its waters a troubled reddish blue. As he walked toward it, the surface boiled and bubbled, then buckled and arced into the air; leaving a pit like a broken boil in the earth. The loch became a moonlike orb that rose skyward, pulling a dripping, twinkling trail of reddish blue water like a tendril of liquefied nerves.

Johnny looked around. The loping, scuttling, gangly, vermillion beetles are almost upon him. They stopped short; making ticking, clicking, chiming noises with their metallic red mandibles.

Before Johnny could run, the ground shuddered. All around him, he saw pools, lochans, and lochs: pulsing, spitting, and spewing into the air until the whole sky stained blood purple; and land and sky inverted. Johnny felt a rippling, pulling, stretching and withering, in his skin and belly, in his bones and brain. The light around him amplified, and soon there was nothing left except its own glaring intensity. Suddenly the glare burnt out.

Johnny walked slowly across a barren moor, as the bloated, low, red sun rose from scattered scarlet clouds. He tried to remember. The moor seemed familiar, teetering on the constant brink of déjà vu. Around the moor lay ancient mountains worn by time, their heads capped in snow like alabaster monuments.

Johnny neared the moor's edge where a marble path began, overhung by lilacs and willows. He stumbled onto its solid mass. He placed old hands on steep steps, and lifted himself up, managing to clamber to the top where a doorway led into the white palace. On his hands and knees he crawled along the stone passageway. Here and there he glimpsed fossils in the marble, as if little animals had fallen into a pit of liquid stone that set hard around them.

Johnny came, at last, to a hole in monument, too tired to move anymore, but he could still see. Outside, he saw a cemetery. His mother and father tended a grave. Where he remembered a little boy standing, there stood a little girl. She looked round, as if sensing his stare. For a moment, a pair of jade eyes peered into his. Then, as if he were simply not there, she looked away. Johnny's sight blurred and fell away into the oblivion of white.

Malcolm Laughton is a speculative fiction writer from Scotland. He's part of the Glasgow Science Fiction Writers Group.

SEA GIRL
by Spike Marlowe

You walk into the Sea Witch's chamber, an aquamarine room with low shimmering lights, surrounded by a wall of glass. Behind the glass is the ocean, full of fish, seaweed, electric eels and small silver sharks.

The Sea Witch sits before you on her blue and green cushions of silk. You have caught sight of her before--she is a common presence in the Skin Trade--but the brief glimpses of her have not prepared you for taking in full on the Sea Witch's presence. For her pearl-pale flesh, glowing blue rimmed irises, shark-sharp teeth. Her right hand made of jellyfish tentacles.

"Come to me, child," she says.

You walk to her, and kneel, your head bowed.

"Look up at me, so I can see you."

You look into her face, and realize her irises are actually tiny floating white jellyfish, the circumference of their bodies glowing as if with blue electricity.

The Sea Witch reaches out to you with her left hand, strokes your jaw, lifts your chin, studies your face. "They tell me you have proven yourself worthy in the Skin Trade."

"Yes, Mistress."

"You have taken the chain mail single-tail. You have taken the cane studded with broken seashells."

You nod your head.

"Show me your scars."

You turn from the Sea Witch, stand, and remove your silken ivory robe. She stands behind you, and you flinch as she runs her fingers along your back, ass, and thighs. "You're not yet healed."

"Not yet, Mistress."

"Are you healed from the six-inch spokes with which they pierced your labia?"

"No, Mistress. Nor from how they then spread me, and beat my clit with the cane of nails, once they'd pierced me."

"Are you willing to take my form of the Skin Trade before you've healed?" the Sea Witch asks.

You turn to her and return to your knees. "Please, Mistress."

"Would you like to see the piece of my skin you will earn if you endure today?"

You nod, and the Sea Witch pushes back her hair from her right shoulder. She rubs her forefinger over the flesh. "This will be yours," she says as she looks into your eyes.

You are flanked by two young women, skin the color of a tropical sea, eyes large, like sea glass, and sea-foam hair falls down their backs. Their lips are like those of fish. "Bathe her, then use the eels."

You are taken from the Sea Witch's chamber and into a small, glowing room, sea shell pink. The Sea Witch's chamber was cool and breezy, but this room is bathwater warm. There is a shower and toilet on one side of the room, and a massage table on the other. A giant bathtub sits in the center of the room.

The Fish Girls coo over you, tell you how soft your human skin is, how beautiful your eyes. They marvel at your marks of the Skin Trade and nuzzle your neck. They draw a bath of salt water and lay out sea sponges. "The water will sting where you've not healed, but it will be warm," they say as they lay out strands of sea weed.

When the tub is filled with sea water, the young women help you step inside. It is true--the salt water stings your marks, and you hiss from the pain. "It will be no worse when the water reaches your other wounds," the Fish Girls promise.

You nod, and allow yourself to process the pain. You breathe through the waves of hurt, and soon you allow the young women to lower you into the warm salt water.

"You are brave," they whisper. "The sea water would make others scream from the pain."

You recline and they gently bathe your torso and legs with the sponges, and lean forward so they can wash your back. A brief cry escapes your lips, but then you breathe in through your nose, briefly hold the breath, exhale through your mouth, riding the pain. When it's time for them to cleanse your sex, you stand, and then they drape you with the sea weed, careful to drape extra strands across your wounds.

"The spikes were very large," they say.

"Very large," you agree.

They help you lie back down in the tub and drape more seaweed between your legs. "You haven't shaved," they observe. "It's very good. You will feel more. You like to feel, don't you?" they ask.

"Yes," you say. "I love to feel."

"We will make you feel," they say. "But first, you must rest and let the water and seaweed do their work."

You close your eyes, and let your body drift in the warm water.

Later, you feel someone stroking your head. You open your eyes to the Fish Girls standing over you. You nod, and they crawl into large tub. They remove the seaweed from your body. Then, each taking a side, they nibble your shoulders with their tiny fish teeth, sucking the dead flesh away from your healing wounds with their mouths. The proceed to nibble and suck your arms down to your fingertips, across your chest, down your sides, over your belly, to your hips and down your legs before they turn you over and travel up your calves and ass and back and neck with their teeth and mouths.

You writhe beneath their mouths, wishing they'd linger over the parts that make your body spasm, the parts that moisten, that want to open to them.

"Thank you," they whisper in your ears when they are done, "for the very delicious meal."

The water has begun to cool, and so the Fish Girls wrap you in a soft, fluffy robe and drain the tub. You lounge in a chair while they refill the tub. When the water is near the top, they ask, "Are you ready for the eels?"

"The eels?" you ask.

"The seawater has ramped your pain levels, but it's not enough for what's to come. The eels will ramp you up further, to prepare you for *her*."

"I'm ready for the eels."

The Fish Girls guide you into the bathtub where you once again recline into the seawater. The salt still twinges on your skin, but it hurts less than it did, and slide into the brief moments of slight pain.

The Fish Girls flip a brass switch on the wall and two holes dilate in the sides of the bathtub. Two eels flow from each of the holes and swirl around in the bathtub. Small flashes of electricity spark from the eels' bodies. You press yourself against the side of the tub. For the first time since entering the Skin Trade you realize there would have been wisdom in asking for what to expect.

The eels twirl in the water, the electricity sparking off their sides and back, jumping off one to another and to another once again before jumping back to the original eel.

"I didn't know they'd be electric," you say.

"But of course," the Fish Girls say.

You look one of the eels in the eye as it swims by you. It stares at you, and for a brief moment you see sentience there, and that's even more horrifying than the thought that the eels were pure animal.

"Move to the middle of the tub," the Fish Girls say, with an authority you haven't heard from them before. You look to them and realize they are now embodying a power they hadn't before. Roles have changed.

You obey them, and push your body through the water, into the middle of the bathtub, into the midst of the eels and their electricity.

"Are they safe?" you ask.

"Nothing we do is safe."

You close your eyes, and you wait.

The first thing you feel is the slick smooth side of an eel as it brushes past your forearm. You flinch and open your eyes. Another eel brushes against your right thigh, another against your waist. An eel flicks its tail against the small of your back, a flick that stings. Another flicks your hip, another your ass, another your thigh. You lower yourself into the water, and the eels continue to flick you with their tails, stinging your breasts, your back. They swim around you, faster and faster, whipping your entire body with their tales.

You begin to moan, and with the escape of your moans, the eels begin to alternate flicking your flesh with their tales with sharp nips from their teeth. You gasp from the pleasure of the sharp and stinging pain.

The eels begin to flick and nip harder and faster, and you find yourself submerging further under the water. Then the Fish Girls are in the seawater with you, holding your head above water so you can breathe.

"Such a good girl," they say. "You're being such a good, good girl." They stroke your hair as the eels bite and spank, bite and spank.

You feel that place between your legs engorge and throb. You move your hands there to stroke, but the Fish Girls take your wrists in their hands and remove them from your groin. Instead, the eels begin to flick and bite that place, making it throb harder and harder.

The Fish Girls lower you back further into the water until your face is barely bobbing atop the water. "Open your legs," the Fish Girls say.

You spread your legs, and the eels begin to slap your clit, and you feel your hips thrusting against their teeth and tails. And then there is a brief shock, a surge of electricity, and your body spasms, but only for a moment. You ride out the spasm, and then there's another shock, more intense this time and you cry out. Another rest, and then another shock, and then you feel an eel enter you.

Electricity radiates through your body. You spasm again, and again. And then, as you feel the eel thrust itself inside of you and the other eels surround your body. Then there's another sharp jolt from your cunt, and then more from the rest of your body, and then you come, and you come, and you come.

The eel exits your cunt, a large, thick, throbbing exit. Then the eels embrace you with their bodies as you come down, the Fish Girls cuddling with you in the water.

Finally, the Fish Girls ask, "Are you ready for her?"

The Fish Girls take you back into the Sea Witch's chambers, once again robed in your ivory silk.

"You look as if you've had the most amazing afternoon," the Sea Witch says. She smiles and leans toward you, leaving a light kiss on your lips.

You bow your head, "Yes, Mistress."

"Are you ready?" the Sea Witch asks.

Your body shudders.

The Sea Witch laughs and her eyes glow more brightly. "Well then, shall we begin?"

The Fish Girls take your robe, tie your hair on top of your head, and buckle your wrists into two cuffs that hang from the ceiling of the Sea Witch's chambers.

The Sea Witch begins by stroking your shoulders and flanks with her left hand. "You have been a very good girl today," she whispers in your ear. Her breath is cool against my neck, like a soft sea breeze. "I'm very impressed with how you've enjoyed my girls, and my eels. This brings me such great pleasure."

Then, she gives your ass a swat. "You like that," she says. "But that's nothing for you, is it? It's not quite enough. That's just saying, "Hello," for you, isn't it?"

"Yes, Mistress."

"I can tell by your wounds that you like it hard. Metal and shells have dug into your flesh. Gouged it. Ripped it. Isn't that true?"

"Yes, Mistress."

"You are used to bleeding for your passion, aren't you? You are used to screaming and crying for it." She gives your ass a sharper swat, and this time she aims for your most recent wounds. You growl; not from the pain--the pain is nothing, especially compared to where you're ramped to after your afternoon--but from her attention. She laughs. "I approve. Once we get going, it will hurt in a way nothing has hurt before. It will go fast, be over quickly. And then I will make it hurt more than you can ever imagine, but then we will make you feel better. Okay, little one?"

"Yes."

She begins to brush her left hand across your back, and then swats your ass on one cheek and then the other. Your wounds burn, and you breathe. Just breathe into it. She begins to slap across your back, and then heavy swats cover your shoulders blades, back and ass. Her hand moves smoothly, and swats sharply. Her hand is more smooth and more sharp than any flogger.

She slows to a stop, and approaches you, pressing her body against your back. She embraces you with her left arm. "How are you feeling?" she asks.

"I am ready for more, Mistress."

She removes her left arm from your chest and walks in front of you and faces you. She displays her right hand, the hand made of jellyfish tentacles. "Do you remember this?"

"Yes, Mistress."

"Are you ready for the most intense pain of your life, child?"

"Yes, Mistress."

She circles around you again, until she is at your back. You feel a cool breeze against your back, and then she strikes--the jellyfish tentacles hit your flesh, with a sting of fire. You cry and writhe under her touch. You feel your hips wanting to grind into her, but she keeps her distance.

She starts to strike you again the momentum faster, the strikes harder, and then there's a change. The pain was intense, but now, suddenly, it's as if tiny acid-filled thorns are piercing your flesh.

You scream and your body jerks, but you will not move away from her. If you move away from her, she might stop. And if she stops, you've lost. Tears flood your face, and the pain sears your back and your ass. And then, as quickly as it begun, she's done. You choke, gasping for breath.

The Fish Girls release you from the cuffs, and you fall to the floor. You open your eyes for a brief moment. "Close your eyes, and cover them. This is going to hurt, and it will be worse if I hit your eyes." You cover your eyes with your hand, and try to calm yourself with your breathing.

The scent of piss and the burning hits at the same time. You scream, a never-ending scream you didn't know your body contained.

"They say that to cure a jellyfish sting, one should pee on the affected flesh. But this is a myth. The truth is, piss on jellyfish stings only intensifies the pain," the Sea Witch says. "Relish the pain, child. This is your baptism."

All you can do is scream and struggle against the hurt.

When it's all over, the Fish Girls take you back into the back room to the bathtub. This time, the Sea Witch crawls into the bath with you, and bathes you herself with warm mineral water. She whispers about what a good girl you are. How proud she is of you. How beautiful and strong you are. She strokes your hair and places her hand over your heart. "Your breathing is slowing, your heart rate is calming."

You smile and melt into the Sea Witches' body. "Ride the waves of pleasure, child. You have earned it. You've been such a very good girl. I'm so very proud of you." The Sea Witch kisses your forehead and continues to bathe your body.

Later, when you are finished bathing and are lying with her upon her silk pillows, she tells you next time she wants to fuck you with her tentacles, how she wants to fuck your ass and hold your heart with her tentacles.

You can't help but wonder what that might be like.

Unlike the previous trades, this Skin Trade is easier than your others. Before, the removal of your skin and graft from your Masters and Mistresses has been the most painful part of your scenes. Now, when the Sea Witch removes flesh from your right shoulder and grafts her own flesh to your body, there is relief from the lessening of pain.

And you will wear her pearl-pale skin with pride.

Spike Marlowe is a busker, performer and a superhero. She is the author of Placenta of Love.

POEM X
by Philip LoPresti

Open her legs.
Read from it like a book.
Drink from the gash
and learn the things that they would never teach you.

Sister Pestilence,
that squirming trashcan slut.
She tastes it with her asshole.
The only way she knows how.
She begs for it with the tip of her tongue.
Her humiliation is a gift to us.
Our compliance, a disease.
She does it this way because it feels good.

Fuck her full of sacrilege
And full of fallen kingdoms.
Stuff her full of books
and read the words from the nesting place.
She is most beautiful
when her insides are brimming with it.

Here I go again.
Into her wetlands.
A rough sort of wandering
through a fractured rush of blood roots blooming.
Blood roots forming.
Gusts of black viscous envelope
the underbelly of her celestial knot.

We will fucking hang for this.
We will pay with our minds and our bodies.

The world is a silent scream
from the mouth of a painted whore,
An anguished Christ awaiting at the end of the hall.

Philip LoPresti is a writer, photographer and musician living in Upstate NY. His books include Haunted Fucking (a book in spasms); I Am Suicide *(in which this poem, "Poem X," appears),* Skull Fuck Abattoir *and* Sick in the Head. *All published by* Dynatox Ministries.

BITVA GRUPPA
by Violet LeVoit

"What's it going to be then, eh?"

There was me, that is Alex, and in the spot where my three droogs, that is Pete, Georgie and Dim, would sit was nobody. Those gloopy mates had got themselves picked up by the millicents and such as it was I is all alone in the Korova Milk bar, nursing my moloko and synthemesc and trying to make up my rasoodock what to do with the evening without them. I told the barkeep to put knives in the moloko, I want to feel that pricky prick, but he viddied me with a squinty eye and slid my moloko over the bar without saying not a word and went back to drying glasses and I should have cracked him a good one over the gulliver for it but I was in a charitable mood and decided to peet and wait for the synthemesc to kick in before kicking the great brachney's face in. I would enjoy it more that way.

But that brachney must have doped me because instead of my gulliver swimming with angels and atomics and the great stereophonic heroin voice of Bog after a few swallows I got dizzy and gloopy, my yahzick thick in my mouth and I could barely hold up my chin to light the cancer between my goobers. O that fucker. He'll be sorry-worry he put that vellocet in Alex DeLarge's gulliver, sorry like that woman and the two girls and the veck in the alley was sorry, horrorshow sorry in a pool of their own krovvy.

But then I was all a tangle trying to rise from the sofa and I spilled my moloko and it spread like a galaxy being birthed across the Korova's tile floor and the cancer dropped from my goobers and fizzled itself out in the moloko spread like a dying star when across the room what do I see but some strange chelloveck one seat over giving me the glazz, viddying me viddy the spreading moloko, giving me a good smirk.

"Looks like you've got a drinking problem," says the chelloveck, and while the room is spinning this veck's face is perfectly clear.

"Milk," he says. "Did you know humans are the only species that routinely drink milk into adulthood? Lactose intolerance is the most common dietary complaint in the world. We lose our ability to digest milk past infancy. The stomach stops making enzymes. We grow new teeth for solid food." He pointed to the moloko on the floor, cancer twixt his fingers like a professor's pointer. "Our adult bodies know we don't need milk. So how come we keep drinking it?"

I had no clue what this veck was saying. I pay no attention to yabbers gobbing on and on while they're on the mesc. He slid in close on the slick seats of the milk bar. He was a tall veck, face battered but kraceevy. And dressed sharp, not like my droogs with their jelly mould and flip horrorshow boots but ragged denim and a shirt what covered with, if you viddied close, hundreds of photos of kraceevy ptitsa doing the in-out in-out with a hundred different vecks, I could barely make out what the veck was saying, so swimming before my eyes was a hundred different cunts and rots and hanks of luscious glory lubbilubbing over and over again.

"Think about it. Every single serving yogurt, every individually wrapped sliced of processed cheese is our refusal of maturity. The entire dairy industry is built on our addiction to our mothers. Our refusal of separation from the world of women. A morphine fix from some eternal tit." The veck fixed me with a viddy so sharp that I looked up from the in-out on his shirt and caught him with a viddy back hoping to scare him something horrorshow but he wasn't scared and instantly I knew I liked him.

"I don't like the moloko. I like what they put in it." I said, meaning the vellocet knives that should go pricky prick and make me jump to do all sorts of ultraviolence.

"You like the permission."

I squinted up my face. "Permission for what?"

"Permission for violence," the veck said, patient like a schoolmaster type. "Permission to indulge your true nature." He pointed to the moloko on the floor. "Permission from Mom."

I said nothing.

The veck reached into his jacket, took out another cancer, lit it, handed it to me and I put it in my rot and smoked deep.

"That's the problem," he said. "Three thousand years ago men like us – men who like violence, who like to hurt, who like to rape – we'd be an evolutionary success. You'd have progeny across the gene pool. Your DNA'd be making the rounds of so many family trees, they'd trace whole races back to you. Now, we sit in bars and drink milk souped up with drugs so we can forget that back on the savannah we'd be supermen. How old are you?"

"Fifteen."

"Fifteen." He shook his gulliver in disdain. "For an Australopithecus, that's middle age. You're genetically primed to go for the gusto, in a society that doesn't need it anymore. Useless as an overbred poodle."

I decided I changed my mind about this veck and wanted to crack him something horrowshow and I turned to the corner of the room like I was thinking and yelped up and came smash down on his head with the empty glass and he just grinned and I was shocked he didn't crumple like the others but I liked it. I liked to see the spraying glass and the moloko rivulets white-pink in the krovvy running down his face.

"That's the spirit," he smiled, and he pulled back and fist me cross the table, sprawling into the mannequins with the moloko fountains in the grudees, crumple me into a heap tangle on the floor.

"Feels good, doesn't it?" he said. "Violence feels good. It's purifying. It's the only thing that can save us. You're lucky enough to be male. Vagina dentata's just a myth. We're the ones whose bodies can be weaponized."

I was sprawled on the floor when he leaned tight to me and said, "You're used to giving pain. But you know what?" He pressed up to me, litso to litso like. "You have to give up. You have to realize that someday you will die. Until you know that? You're useless."

I fist his face again and he took it with radosty in his glazzers and said, "That's it. I want you to hit me as hard as you can." And I did, again and again, and each time he sucked it up and the krovvy flowed sticky and dark across his face and across my fist and stuck my fingers together and splattered on my whites and he gave me a good go and then laid into me, fist me again and again in the face and it felt so pure radosty I thought, is this what they felt? The woman and the two girls and the veck in the alley and everyone else who crossed my path when I was prickly with the mesc ready for the twenty-and-one. And the truth reared up. I didn't care what they felt and I never did. All I cared was right now, with that veck's fist beating me in the face and my own nose popping, krovvy running hot down my goobers tasting metal like that I was pure like a needle run red through a red hot flame.

Then the barkeep sees what a mess us droogs are making of his bar and he runs over but the veck cracks him a good one and he drops to the ground and I kick his guttiwuts until he spits up krovvy bile and lays still and and as we run out of the bar into Boothby Avenue, that merzky tunnel where me and my droogs beat that doddery starry schoolmaster type just last week, andI ask finally "What's your name?" and the veck says "Tyler." And I am fairly busting with radosty who needs me gloopy droogs when I've got this veck who loves the ultraviolence like I do. And I say, "O my Tyler let us run the night and find us some of the old in-out" and Tyler shakes his head and says "Still looking for women to solve your problems."

And I'm to ask what he means, I'm so itched to get going and find some ptista, that krovvy round my rot got me a pan-handle up against the inside of the old jelly mould when he presses me up to the alleyway wall and hisses in my ear "You have to trust me."

His rookers crawled around the old jelly mould around my crutch and I stiffened thinking no gollyboy is going to take me and I headbutted him and ran but he was too quick like, he tackled me and pressed me again up the wall and now I knew I was spoogy in over me gulliver and opened my rot to creech but he pressed his rot over mine and I jumped when I felt his yahzick crest over mine so stunned was I, I forgot to creech for help. I'm no gollyboy I thought. I'm not I'm not I'm not but Bog help me no ptitsa kisses like a fine young malchickiwick and O my pan-handle did not mind one bit what flavor rot kissed mine.

"See?" Tyler said. When his rookers went round my jelly mould this time I did not stop him, not when his fingers crept round my neezhnies down to my yarblockos that jumped under his touch neither. "Who needs women?" he said. "We waste our lives accumulating things we don't want trying to impress them. But we've got everything right here." I did not listen as my glazzies were rolling up in the back of my head. I liked what he did to my pan-handle fine but I had better ideas.

"I like the ultraviolence," I said. "I mean, the in-out is horrorshow but I like it best when there's a bit of krovvy to go with." And Tyler smirked and said, "Don't worry, there'll be plenty of that" and flipped me over and wrapped his arm round my shiyah so my chin buried into his elbow whilst he held me tight like a scotina to be branded and pulled down my pants to just below and I could feel his pan-handle up between the sharries and as he pushed inside hot sweat ran down my litso and I felt a surge of radosty I only felt once before, whilst listening for the first time to the great 9th of Ludwig Van.

And then the moloko fog in me gulliver cleared and the chokehold round my shiyah melted away and there I was in the alleyway, my trousers down to my sharries like I was about to dung but got caught. Nobody was there. O when my droogs get out of the Staja O what fun we will have. I was cured all right.

Violet LeVoit is a writer and film critic whose work has appeared in numerous film, horror and bizarro anthologies. She is the author of the short short story collections *I Am Genghis Cum* (2011) and *I'll Fuck Anything that Moves and Stephen Hawking* (2014, both Fungasm Press). Her film criticism has appeared in the *Baltimore City Paper, PressPlay.com, TurnerClassicMovies.com, FilmThreat,com, Allmovie. com*, and *The Little Black Book: Movies* (Cassell Illustrated) among others. Originally from Baltimore, she now lives in Philadelphia.

OKCupid
by Anna Suarez

A slut loves her blowjobs,
Her liquor, her body, her
Freedom.

A slut can stay out
And embrace the wild night,
Blow kisses across the street
When her bus arrives.

She is always
The one spoken of.

But *her* words, the possible
Ecstasies, Unarmed, enmeshed, em-
battled sorrows, her truths,
unsung songs, buried
beneath a bed of
lilacs, nights

spent reapplying lipstick,
hovering over tumblers of water,
mugs of tea, glasses of wine,
A canvas sail drifting between
sentences, finding lost socks
under beds, putting earrings
back in my purse because I
couldn't find the back. (He
never looked, anyhow.)

Now my tea comes. The aroma
glides across my pours: herbs,
flowers, honey. Black

eyes watching my little sips, done
in fear of smudging red-velvet
lipstick, wondering if only
Living could be

herbs, flowers, honey.

I spread my legs during the first
ten minutes of 'Lost in Translation;'
Scarlett Johansson telling Bill Murray:
"I'm stuck," & I'm wiping salt slivers
of ocean from my cheeks as you
hold my hips beneath the
waves.

PORN STARS AND PECCADILLOS
by Laura Roberts

I seem to attract a certain kind of client on a regular basis. Businessmen on benders, sure, but also something darker, something weirder. Montreal, according to most Americans, is a hotbed of sexual activity, but for our friends in the lower 48 it's actually best known for its booming porn industry. This was news to me, delivered by my first aspiring porn star-cum-client, Randy.

"Don't y'all shoot pornos up here somewhere?" he asked me, ever so subtly. We were walking down Ste-Catherine, and he had spotted some of the signs indicating that the street would be blocked off tomorrow morning for another film shoot. Montreal doubles for New York City, LA and even Toronto on a fairly regular basis, as a weak Loonie has made for strong American dollars—along with some fabulously star-quality buying power. I think George Clooney may have passed us as Randy gaped, but Canadians aren't the type to flock around stars and clamor for autographs. Just another perk of living in this city, especially when you're famous. Or infamous.

"Of course. But it's not like they're open set, if you know what I mean."

Randy pouted. "But you must know someone," he pressed.

"You mean you'd like to meet some of the actresses?"

He blew air out of his mouth, ruffling his hair impatiently. "Not exactly."

I pondered this for a moment, wondering if he meant what I thought he meant. "So… you'd like to do a casting call?"

"I'm ready to rock 'n' roll, baby. This six-shooter's ready to blow!" he crowed. He cupped his crotch to indicate his *pistola*.

I smiled indulgently and racked my brain for a contact that wouldn't be offended by my bringing this Texas lunk to their set—or worse, their home turf HQ.

"It doesn't have to be right now," he reassured me. "In fact, I was thinking of getting a bite to eat first. Say, do y'all have those places where you can eat sushi off a live nude girl?"

I rolled my eyes at the request, but quickly plastered my smile back on. At least this query was run-of-the-mill. "Sure, Randy. Right this way."

As we ambled down Ste-Catherine towards the sexy sushi spot, I scrolled through my address book in search of an impromptu porn director with a passably professional looking camera. My pervy friend Ian had always wanted to start a porn company, but he was in it more for the chance to fuck a few naïve starlets, and I doubted he'd take kindly to any requests to indulge a big-dicked American in search of porno pussy. *Think, Frankie, think!*

I almost laughed out loud when her name finally appeared in my scattered mind: Honey Lee. Of course! I texted her as Randy and I turned into the unassuming sushi shop, conveniently deserted at high noon. After chatting in Japanese with the proprietor, who knew all about her clients' particular fetishes and fantasies and could tell just by looking at him that Randy was going to want the tiniest, tightest little Asian she could rustle up, I switched back to English to tell Randy it'd be a couple of minutes. Meanwhile, we could drink tea in the parlor. When the geisha-girl in a tight-fitting, short-skirted kimono finally came to accompany us to the tearoom, he looked like he was already about to bust a nut.

As the geisha giggled and fawned over Randy, allowing him to squeeze her diminutive cheeks, I got a *ping!* on my phone. Honey Lee had texted back, saying my proposal sounded like fun, and she had some free time in her schedule in the early evening. Score!

The geisha-girl departed, and Randy turned his attention back to me. "So, what's the good word?"

"You're in luck. Ms. Honey Lee is free this evening."

"Honey Lee? Sounds… sweet." He licked his lips.

"Oh, she's about as sweet as southern tea," I assured him.

Honey was originally a stripper, like most of us ladies in the biz. She got bored with the gig a bit quicker than most, but she'd always enjoyed the after-parties, with plenty of drugs and booze to go around—along with plenty of free-spirited sex workers willing to swing any which way on their time off. She was one of the few, the proud, the ladies who simply love to fuck. And since Honey enjoyed her work, she sure as hell didn't mind being paid for it when she was in the mood for love.

Oddly enough, the payment was the real turn-on for Honey, as the more they paid her, the more she wanted them. But working in the clubs, where her profession lent itself more to the tease than sealing the deal, she wanted more. Lots more.

So, she saved up a couple thousand, bought a run-down loft in what was then the unpopular part of town, spruced the place up with her own unique style (some might say a cross between Betsey Johnson and the Marquis de Sade), transforming the three-story house into her fabulous living quarters and brand new studio space. The home of HoneyPot Productions was born.

These days, she's the head honcho, performing all her own stunts as well as directing up-and-cummers in her boudoir. She hosts a daily show on her website, with a revolving cast of guys, gals, transsexuals and ex-lovers starring in what amounts to a sexual soap opera, serialized. Subscribers have all-access passes, while those who are just browsing can check out quick clips of Honey's O-face, as well as work-friendly episodes of her shopping for groceries in a tiny negligee, among other hilarious "hot girl in too little clothing" trailers filmed on location around town. The lesbians love her, as do straight men that haven't clued into her personal preferences, so it's win-win all around.

"So… she's going to need to see my bratwurst, right?" Randy asks, giving me an entirely inappropriate wink.

"She might. Ms. Lee works in mysterious ways," I say, trying to gie her a little leeway. Who knows what she's actually got in store for this wannabe Ron Jeremy?

"I can do tricks with it," he stage whispers.

"Tricks? What kind of tricks?" Now I'm just confused. You can do tricks with your penis?

"Yeah. Have you ever heard of 'Puppetry of the Penis'?" he asks me, looking very serious indeed. It appears we have hit upon one of Randy's true passions.

"No, I can't say that I have," I admit.

"Well… they're these Australian fags—at least, I think they're fags… anyway, they can make their cocks into different animals and stuff."

"You mean like shadow puppets?"

"Yeah, exactly!" He beams like we are really connecting, and I start to realize what a weirdo I've got on my hands. He sits around shaping his cock into animals? Like, beyond the typical trouser snake we all know and love?

"Oh. That sounds… interesting," I say.

I have no idea why I said that. Puppets made out of someone's penis don't sound the least bit interesting, when you really stop and think about it. The only shape I am particularly interested in a penis being is engorged and penis-shaped. Bring me your hard-ons and I'll show you a lady that loves to suck. But I digress.

"Yeah! It's pretty fun. I can make a tiger, a lion and a panther," he says. He doesn't seem to realize these are all, essentially, the same animal. Particularly as far as penis puppetry is concerned.

"Awesome," I say, racking my brain for another line of questioning, or a train to derail this rather disturbing thought process. I surreptitiously text Honey that the client she's going to be receiving has a thing for wiener wangs, among other odd predilections.

I wonder if Honey is going to really want to deal with this guy. He's definitely moving into territory bordering on the bizarre. I've got plenty of experience dealing with all manner of perverts and posers, so it's odd to realize that this is new territory for me.

"And I've been thinking about branching out into different scenes…" Randy is saying. I tune him out to concentrate on Honey's texts, nodding my head at all the right moments, or whenever he appears to be pausing for effect.

Honey has texted back reassurances that she can handle any damn man who wants to "get all up in her grill," and I believe her. She's seen it all, by now. Even the likes of Randy LeRaunch.

Our sushi girl finally makes her appearance, shutting Randy up for a moment as he gawps over her tiny, thin form. She climbs onto our low-slung table and arranges her body carefully. The geisha assists, placing a pillow underneath her head, and the sushi chef (who must be completely affronted by the way in which his culinary masterpieces are being treated) lends a hand in the art of arrangement. By the time they two of them are finished, our sushi girl looks like she's had a line of ikebana experts arrange an unusual bouquet of fish across her slender form.

Randy is salivating now, a Pavlovian mutt. I'm not sure which excites him more, the sushi or the girl obscured by his meal. A little of column A, a little of column B, I suppose.

The girl is stiff as a board, with tiny mounds rising from her chest creating miniature Mt. Sushi peaks. The sushi itself looks relatively inedible, at least to my eyes. I'm not exactly a connoisseur, but I do know that sushi rice ought to hold together under pressure—and I'd include being exposed to a woman's naked flesh as "pressure," wouldn't you?

Randy doesn't care about any of that. He is hungrily gobbling up the bits of raw fish, caviar and rice in an effort to expose more of the girl's body. He isn't even bothering with the delicate cups of soy sauce and wasabi. It seems as though his plan of attack is to strategically remove all fish from her target areas: tits, crotch, belly button. What he'll do next is a mystery to me. I excuse myself from the table and head to the ladies' room as he plows his way towards total exposure.

In the cool, enclosed space of the ladies' room, I close the toilet seat, heave a sigh and sit down. I think about having a cigarette, but it's a little too early in the day for that indulgence. Instead, I pick up my phone and message Honey again. "This guy's a freak. He's gobbling an entire sushi bar off a geisha right now and thinks you're going to want to judge him by the size of his dick. What should I tell him?" I write.

She responds almost instantaneously: "Whatever he wants to hear. You're the boss!"

I stand up and look at myself in the mirror. How have I gotten myself into this situation, anyway? Why am I giving stupid little sex tours to idiots like this, wasting my potential and my life instead of doing something useful or brilliant? I'm the boss, but the boss of what?

"You're the mayor of shit," I whisper to my morose face. Then I bare my teeth like a wolf about to strike.

Get out now, a little voice is nagging me, somewhere at the base of my skull. Could it be my conscience?

Shut up, I think. I have to finish what I started. I grab my lipstick and re-apply my war paint, square my shoulders back and give myself my favorite pep talk.

"You are the queen of your own destiny. You have chosen this life. You are responsible for all of your actions, and you can determine all of your outcomes. You are not a victim, and you cannot be stopped when you set your mind to something. Remember: It's not who is going to let you, but who is going to stop you. Fuck this noise. Fuck these clients. Fuck the world. You are here to do the job the best you can, and you will not fail. Grab life by the balls and squeeze. You can do it. You are a motherfucking warrior queen. FIGHT!"

I return my lipstick and phone to my purse, take a deep breath to steel my resolve, and return to the dining area.

As I step back into the room, I notice that Randy's cheeks are stuffed full of sushi. He resembles nothing more than an overgrown chipmunk, scavenging for the last acorns of the season. I almost laugh aloud at the sight, but manage to maintain my composure.

I'd better be in charge here, I think to myself. *This fool certainly can't handle any truthiness about the realities of the situation.*

"Does your client need any other services?" Madame Khan asks me in Japanese.

"We're on our way to another appointment," I demure.

She nods and hands me the bill. I surrender my credit card and bow politely, and she returns the gesture.

"Come back anytime, Francesca-san," she murmurs, floating off like a lotus flower on the gentle gust of a summer breeze.

For the privilege of experiencing this meal, Randy has incurred a $450 tab. And that didn't even include drinks. This business is getting more expensive every day. Maybe it's about time I thought about getting out of the game.

For the record, there are most certainly rules about eating sushi off a naked girl's body. Here they are, in case you've been wondering:

146

1. No touching, no tasting. Except when it comes to the sushi.
2. No mistaking a gal's nether regions for "sushi," just because you think they both "taste like fish."
3. Eating is the only activity allowed within the dining area.
4. No pictures permitted.
5. All sushi must be consumed on the premises.
6. There is a 50-cent surcharge for each sushi roll not eaten, to prevent wasteful over-ordering.
7. Extra services may be ordered via the waitress, including massages and happy endings. These will all be performed in separate rooms, for sanitary, as well as legal, purposes.
8. If a geisha or server says no, *she means no!!* Violators of this rule will be immediately ejected from the premises, no questions asked. Your credit card can and will be charged for associated damages.
9. A credit card must be surrendered to the shop owner prior to entering the scene. Government-issued ID must also be shown, and photocopies will be made in order to prevent any violent activities.

And never forget Chris Rock's rule of thumb: There's NO SEX in the Champagne Room. Nor the Saké Room, for that matter.

Randy and I cab it over to Honey's place, after he freshens up at his hotel. Both of us are nervous, having never been through a pornographic casting call, much less the rigors of a DIY porn star's directorial whims. I feel I'm in slightly better a position than Randy is; at least I've met Honey before, and I know she's a good person that I can trust. But we work in the same industry, and we have a history, if not a common interest.

Randy, on the other hand, has no such guarantees. We could, in theory, rob this man blind and throw him to the wolves. Or the Hell's Angels, if we saw fit. And I think he is finally, somewhere in the murky recesses of his amphibian brain, realizing this danger. His eyes are blinking much more rapidly, at any rate, and his breathing is quick and shallow. He's scared.

Who wouldn't be?

I put a reassuring palm on his upper thigh and coo softly, "Don't be nervous. Honey Lee's a true professional."

"That's what I'm a-worried about," he chokes out.

"Randy, you know you're the man," I soothe.

"Frankie… what if… I mean, what if she don't think it's big enough?"

"Oh, Randy, don't be silly," I chuckle. I catch the cab driver's eyes in the rear-view and arch an eyebrow at him, as if to say *Keep your trap shut.*

"I mean, I know my six-shooter's ready for anything, but… well, what are y'all used to up here?" he asks, nervously turning to face me.

"Montreal women are just like American women," I assure him. "It's not the size of your boat; it's the motion of your ocean."

"I was afraid you'd say that," he mutters.

"Randy, you're a regular stud! You told me about all your exploits. The preacher's wife, the small-town girls you sweet-talked into an orgy… surely you're not worried about a little ol' camera?" I give him a playful punch on the shoulder.

"Ms. Parker, can I tell you something in confidence?" he asks, looking very worried indeed.

"Anything, Randy," I say, stroking his arm.

"I… well, I lied about all that. I've never done any of those things. Although I've certainly dreamed about 'em." He looks like he is sincerely on the verge of breaking into tears. I can hardly believe it; this big galoot is confessing his sexual sins to me like I'm a priest able to dole out pardons! I swallow the urge to laugh, and try to think of an appropriately somber response to his dilemma.

"Well, Randy, we all embellish the truth a bit to impress the opposite sex," I begin. "But isn't the point that you *thought* you could do those things, even if you never actually *did* them?"

He ponders this silently for a few moments. The taxi driver doesn't make eye contact with me, steering us ever closer to our destination, our destiny.

"Well… I suppose that makes sense," he finally allows.

"There you go! You've got to think positive, Randy. You've got it going on. Just look at you! You're tall, you're buff, you've got a gorgeous smile and a cute Texan accent—"

"Whaddya mean 'Texan accent'!" he yelps.

"Just like in *Midnight Cowboy*," I murmur, more to myself than to him.

"Oh, god, she'll hate me!" he howls, pushing his face into his lap.

"No, no," I soothe, patting him on the back. "Honey is a very multicultural kind of girl. And she loves a good accent."

Laura Roberts writes about sex, travel, writing and ninjas - though not necessarily in that order. She's the founding editor of the literary magazine Black Heart, *the San Diego chapter leader for the Nonfiction Authors Association, and she leg-presses sumo wrestlers in her free time. She lives in an Apocalypse-proof bunker in sunny SoCal with her artist husband and their literary kitties, and can be found online at Buttontapper.com*

SIGN OF THE TIMES
by Carole Johnstone

When I was fifteen, the dog-heads came back. I had no idea they'd even been gone. My best friend was one of them. He's the only friend I've ever had. His name was Vinnie.

Vinnie lived in the zoo out by the docks. They weren't called zoos then; I forget what they *were* called in the beginning: holding or assessment centres, some crap like that. The docks were a good place for one at any rate; they'd only just infilled the East Dock and the big renovations hadn't got underway, at best there were half a dozen small business units on Bonnington and Seafield, and the first lot of fat wallets who'd been building 'affordable' housing on Lindsay Road had gone bust. The docks were far enough away from the city that no one had to see it or live close by it, which was the main thing – probably the only thing.

Vinnie was second-gen. There were a lot of them in the zoo. Because it was one of the first in the country – in any country – they were either too slow or too panicked to segregate and/or neuter, so pretty soon there were plenty third-gens too. If I'm honest, I don't know much about the beginning; I was too young and carefully sullen back then and there was far too much shouting. Sometimes, when I think back, the shouting's all I can remember: mostly dad and his market stall cronies, pissed on grateful fury.

A lot of those 'precautionary measures' employed elsewhere didn't work anyway. Net searches showed library images of zoos that looked like private hospitals or slum ghettos; they were either serenely aseptic or hysterically appalled, not that you could trust anything you found on there anyway. Dad had his own theory: Shit Always Rises to the Top. Which I guess was his way of saying nature always finds a way.

I probably never would have met Vinnie or Millie or Vinnie's dad or Pipe Cleaner – or any dog-head at all – if it wasn't for dad though. Even after the very worst of it was over (distilled into better religious, xenophobic, or outraged sound bites as soon as it was), he pretended that it wasn't so, but he was lying. He tried to rewrite our past even as the world rewrote its future, but that's dad for you. When he'd first found out how much the council was offering to pay folk for caretaking down at the docks, he jacked in his stall and had us both moved into one of the few completed housing blocks on Lindsay Road within weeks. He knows that; he hates that.

It was a weird place. Even ignoring the flat-roofed warren of the zoo itself, the docks were a half-finished wasteland surrounded by medieval walls: the spires and towers of the city to its south; the dirty, sandy flats of the firth to its north. For a teenager used to the lights and bustle of a city – albeit a teenager more antisocial than most and a side of the city poorer than all – it was an alien place, a vacant strip on the edge of land. Full of ghosts and un-exorcised fear. Sometimes I could feel that fear creeping over fort walls and redundant brick stacks shone silver by the moon. On those nights, the dog-heads howled until sunrise.

Dad's caretaking involved a little more than the security guarding he'd been expecting. The zoo was a former seamen's mission, though that was only its hub – most of it was prefab, hollow-walled extension. From the sky it must have looked like a giant and ugly spider web radiating sticky threads. The dog-heads lived in knocked-through spaces – ten to fifteen a room – with chicken wire fronts, mounted and orange-glowing electric heaters and spring-latch door corridors, segmented into three two by six foot spans like big cat enclosures, for the safety of the caretakers. I guess that's how the zoos got their name (they all eventually followed the same generic layout), that and the live feed cameras switched on during more interesting moments: the introduction of new residents, feeding time, territorial fights and sneaky shags.

During the day, most of the dog-heads were allowed out into a vast communal area known as the Playground. It was a flat and concrete expanse covering better than five hundred yards square between the rear of the zoo and the Sands. There was nothing in it. No seats, no tables. Nothing but concrete. But that was just in the beginning. Vinnie told me once that he didn't mind it – didn't mind any of it, because there were far, far worse places for dog-heads to be – but though I believed him then, I'm not sure I do now. I might not remember much about the politics and the logistics and the crap that folk spouted to justify means to ends –those days you weren't allowed to call a spade a spade, as if calling it anything else made it anything other than a fucking spade (apartheid, segregation, even quarantine were swearwords you couldn't apply to immigrants of any kind, even those with the same kind of head as yours) – but I knew what dad and his cronies had done every time a new trader had moved in with the potential to undercut them. Folk never like change; they never embrace different. They just hate it.

--o0O0o--

The first time I saw Vinnie, he was nosing inside one of the big dumper bins at the back of the Lindsay Street flats. It was the first time I'd seen any dog-head up close, but I wasn't frightened. I felt embarrassed for him – embarrassed that I'd seen him scavenging in our rubbish. I kind of wandered half-backwards towards him, whistling into the icy, starlit sky loud enough to give him a chance to stop what he was doing. By the time I turned around, he'd moved away from the bin and was wiping the back of his fingers across his wet nose.

"Alright?" It was more than most folk got from me, even after weeks of vague acquaintance.

Vinnie blinked. His black pupils were huge, and I knew he was seeing a lot more of me than I was of him. He had a broad head with a pronounced brow and a blunt muzzle. Flat floppy ears hung close to his head and dropped to the angle of his jaw. Even in the dark I could tell that his hair was pale gold, and it was this more than anything that convinced me he was a Lab Retriever. I could tell he was second-gen because he was short, nearly hunched (second-gens had a ligament connecting their first thoracic vertebrae to the axis bone of their necks), and he walked mostly on his toes, his feet small and tight.

152

We stood in the featureless backyard of the Lindsay Road flats, blinking at each other, breathing twin fogs of November breath that met and mingled by the thrown light of my and dad's living room on the first floor. I remembered dad telling me that second-gens were savage inbreds that never got a pass into the Playground. I remembered him telling me that they could barely speak a word of recognisable English.

"My name is Pete."

Vinnie made a noise inside his blunt nose that I only recognised as a snort when he began beating hard against his chest with his fists. "Me Vinnie." He showed me the whites of his eyes. "Mofo."

I bared my teeth in what might have been a startled grin. "How d'ye speak?"

"How the fuck do *you* speak?"

After that exchange, we just blinked and breathed at one another some more. Vinnie was the first to cave in. He gave me one of those long, wet blinks again. "You watch the derby Saturday? Shitstorm. Linesman was a Proddy bastard."

"Ye've no' got a TV." This was my way of telling Vinnie that I understood; that I was no more surprised by the topic of his conversation than by his nonchalant escape from the zoo. A big part of me had already decided that the difference between us and the dog-heads ran far deeper than mere appearance. I was right about that as it goes – just not in the childish, supernatural ways I'd thought.

"Yeah we do. And a radio." He caught my eye and there was more defiance in it than threat. I wasn't about to tell dad though; the idea hadn't even occurred to me. Ammunition was something dad was never in short supply of.

"Ye're a Hibee?"

Another long, wet blink. "Ayee."

"It's aye."

He looked away from me for the first time, but I caught the gnash of his long teeth as he huffed and muttered foggier breath. "Aye."

I watched the light from the flats bounce off the shine of his short-haired crown and felt my own teeth run against the inside of my lips. "Linesmen are allus Proddy bastards."

After that I showed a lot more interest in dad's job – enough that he eventually let me accompany him on the night shifts when no one else was on duty. He might have thought that it was because I wanted to spend time with him; I *knew* he saw it as an excuse to kick back in his portacabin and have a *wee swally* on duty (though very rarely were his swallys ever wee). He'd send me off on his patrols, his rifle slung over my shoulder, his rounds rattling inside my combats, his company instructions ringing in my ears: gun stock against the chicken wire to shut them up; tazer through the chicken wire to really shut them up; .30 carbine cartridges to really, really shut them up; a ludicrously heavy under-slung grenade launcher to presumably shut up the entire place should the need ever arise. I didn't care about any of it. If dad had already chambered a round, I'd take it out, and instead I'd shine the rifle's light-sight into the darkness of the chicken wire cages. I always said hello first; I didn't want them to think I was a dick.

Vinnie lived in Cage Two, along with his dad and several brothers. They all had Bulldog-like features and stockier bodies, and I was pretty certain that Vinnie was actually related to none of them, but as they were the only dog-heads who would even look at me never mind speak to me, I never said so.

Vinnie's dad looked old. His eyes were big and yellow, and they often leaked into the jowly folds around his snout. He had a lot of scars too: some on his neck, but most on his torso and flanks. The dog-heads weren't given clothes in any zoo; I never knew if they wanted them or not.

Vinnie's dad didn't say anything to me for weeks, but he always watched from a corner whenever Vinnie and me talked, which we did every chance we got. I liked Vinnie; he was funny as fuck and he never once looked at me the way the rest of them did. Like I'd helped put them there. He asked me about my life as if he didn't care that his was shitter, for which I had some affinity. And I guess, maybe – and not so deep down either – that was my main reason for being there, for liking him. At least in the beginning.

The first night I broke Vinnie out, one of his brothers caught us inside the last spring-latch corridor. I had a moment of panic where I thought he was going to escape too – he was a mean looking bastard and his skin was always puckered, bristled, like he was about to go postal – but instead he told us to watch ourselves and get back within the hour. Vinnie told him to fuck off.

Once we'd made it out of the cage and then onto the wasteland, I wasn't sure where to go, what to do. It felt very important that we do something, but the docks were barren, soulless, and mostly lightless.

Vinnie snorted white fog through his nose. "Thanks for this."

My breakout had been clumsy, we'd been caught before we'd even managed to get out of the cage, and I was pretty certain that Vinnie could and did come and go as he pleased on his own, so I snorted white fog back.

"Let's go to the firth." Vinnie said.

"The firth?"

Vinnie showed his teeth. "I like the water."

We headed out along the infilled east dock because both the guards' portacabin and Lindsay Road were west. There were no lights at all along the east dock, so we had the rifle's light-sight and little else to help us pick our way between the open oil-storage pipes that ran along its length. My feet scuffed and ground gravel; Vinnie's made no sound at all.

"What's that?"

I stopped and turned back around, wheeling the narrow beam up and over Vinnie, and then across the circular wall of the building he'd stopped at. "The Martello Tower. They built it durin' the Napoleonic War tae defend the entrance tae the harbour."

"Yeah?"

When I shone the rifle's light over Vinnie's face, his mouth was open, long tongue exposed. I turned the light back onto the smooth wall. "It's a tunnel vault round a central pillar. It's got a trefoil gun-emplacement on the roof – looks fuckin' amazin' on Google maps."

"It's not very high."

I grinned, coming up alongside Vinnie's shoulder. "It's half-buried. Ye know, I mean it used tae be bigger. A lot bigger. A' ae this—" I swung my light around us and then back to the tower, "used tae be The Black Rocks. It was offshore, ye ken?"

"The Black Rocks?"

"Aye. An' then the outer harbour was built o'er the top ae them, and y'know, here we are. Dry, ugly fuckin' land."

Vinnie didn't look at me. He looked at the tower, and then at the concrete under our feet. "The Black Rocks."

I smiled, shrugged, not really understanding why Vinnie gave a shit, but being glad that he did – that my breaking him out had been worth that at least.

We kept on walking along the eastern dock, its long finger narrowing and narrowing, the coastal wind growing and growing, until we were standing at the red-flashing land buoy at its tip, our breath and voices whipped away into black space.

"What's out there?"

I played the light-sight over dark, choppy water. "Burntisland, Kinghorn, Kirkcaldy further oot. The firth narrows west towards The Ferry, the bridges and all the rest ae it."

Vinnie kept looking east. "And there?"

"North Berwick. Anstruther. And then nothin'."

"Nothin'?"

I shone the light-sight on his face, but he didn't turn, didn't even blink. "Nothin'. The North Sea. Fuck all. Nothin'."

Vinnie sat down, crossing his legs. I was just about ready to go back, because it was cold – really fucking cold – but I did the same instead, pulling my jacket higher about my neck, ignoring the waft of icy wind inside my combats, the trapped howl of it inside the bigger confines of the firth's gullet. We didn't speak for ages; long enough for me to turn the light-sight off.

"Where d'ye come frae?" I'd never asked him that before – I'd never asked any of them that – but in the dark and the roaring quiet it was easier to do.

Vinnie didn't answer for a long time, and when he did his voice was low, almost too quiet to hear. "I can't talk about that."

"A'right." I turned the light-sight on again out of little more than twitchy fingers. The firth bit back blacker, angrier. "There was a sea battle in the middle of the harbour once," I said.

"Yeah?" Vinnie looked back over his shoulder at the calmer water behind us. "When?"

I shrugged in the dark. "Seventeenth century, I think." It had been 1622, but I didn't want to sound like a dick. "A Spanish frigate belongin' tae Philip IV and commanded by a Don Pedro de Vanronz had docked for provisions–"

"Don Pedro de Vanronz?" Vinnie snorted, knocking his shoulder hard against my own. "Fucking hell, it's you!"

"Ye want tae hear this or whit?" I growled, but in the dark I was smiling.

"Aye."

"One night two warships drop anchor right near the frigate. They're both Dutch right, and the Dutch and the Spanish absolutely fuckin' hate each other, so the minute the sun comes up they start fightin', firin' broadside after broadside at each other an' then hand tae hand combat wi' swords on the decks. Bullets and cannonballs are hittin' hooses and walls and folk too stupit tae stay away frae the piers; the city council cannae get them tae stop so they bring a whole battery ae guns doon frae the castle, but afore they can use them, the Dutch ships drive the Spanish frigate out ae the harbour and ontae the Black Rocks, where they board her and burn her tae a crisp." I turned the light-sight onto Vinnie. He was looking at me, the markings like eyebrows sitting high on his brow. His eyes were shining wet. He didn't look even a little bit cold. I grinned. "And then they fucked off back tae Holland."

"No more Don Pedro."

"Guess no'."

"You know a lot of shit," Vinnie said, and I felt an embarrassed surge of pride.

"It's shite," I corrected.

"Shite," Vinnie experimented, the sh- sounding strange filtered through his teeth. "That mean the same thing?"

I chuckled, thinking of my dad. "Sometimes." I flashed the light-sight on and off against the choppy firth.

"It's not really the water I like," Vinnie said, and when I turned the light back onto him instead, he was looking north, his snout in long profile. "It's the space."

I didn't answer him because the opposite was true for me. The space beyond the docks frightened the crap out of me even though I hated everything inside it too.

"D'you swim?"

"Kinda'." I shrugged, looked out at the water and then back at Vinnie. I grinned again. "Doggy paddle."

Vinnie laughed; I realised it was the first time I'd heard him do it. "Fuck off."

I put down the rifle, letting its narrow beam illuminate the concrete between us. "D'ye smoke?"

"Aye."

It took me more than half a dozen attempts to get dad's rollie lit and its tobacco was sour, but after a few unenthusiastic puffs I handed it over to Vinnie. I didn't watch him smoke it out of courtesy; I wasn't sure he could.

After a few seconds of silence, his voice sounded hoarse. "Ye no' got anythin' stronger?"

I didn't. But the next night, I did.

--oO0o--

It rained a lot that winter. You never got much snow on the coast, but the temperature often dropped below minus ten and the winds were ferocious. That year they were even worse. There were flood and gale warnings and sub-zero alerts just about every other night. Our old tenement in Gorgie was condemned because of subsidence that had rolled over from the wet summer; whole streets were bulldozed and cordoned off for eventual repair. Large swathes of the city became uninhabitable.

The dog-heads suffered as badly; dad said that dogs were outdoor beasts, so it didn't matter. One night between Christmas and

Hogmanay, when he and his fellow caretakers were getting pissed on homebrew in our flat, the North Sea wind howling through hidden and uninsulated spaces, I asked him if we could move the dog-heads inside the mission for a few weeks.

"Ye dinna ask me that again, okay?" He blinked eyes shot red with smoke and booze and too little sleep. "Dogs are dogs are fuckin' dogs."

"They're no' dogs."

He shoved me hard against the kitchen sink, rattling dirty crockery and crony laughter. "Dogs are dogs are fuckin' dogs, son, an' I dinna' want tae hear ye sayin' any different in company, a'right?"

I breathed in his stinking breath, and I took the hard edge of the countertop digging into my back and his knee crushing my left bollock because I was nearly old enough for him to legitimately kick me out and there was still nowhere else for me to go.

He planted the heel of a flat palm hard against my breastbone before letting me move again. "Fuckin' mammy's boy."

--o0O0o--

There wasn't much he or the rest of his new cronies could do about all the charity folk though. They had been protesting online and in the city for months, but when the weather got really bad they began picketing the docks close to Lindsay Road and the Albert Basin. This was, of course, bad PR for the company, and so dad and the rest of them had to let them in, show them about, pretend to give a shite.

The charity folk handed out blankets and sleeping bags and pallet-loads of dog food and bottled water. Some of them sang songs; others prayed on their knees or in windswept huddles. Vinnie told me that the worst ones tried to talk to them through the chicken wire. He said that some of them didn't just want to save their souls – they wanted to save the world. I told him he should milk the bastards for all they were worth; every Sunday I got a three course meal in the old hall next to the Parish Kirk just by looking like I needed one.

When one of the big networks came down to film a documentary, I followed dad to the zoo because I knew he wouldn't be able to tell me to fuck off when we got there. The film crew recorded the charity folk handing over more pallet-loads of crap to the caretakers close to the zoo's chicken wire walls, and then they began interviewing random people in enthusiastic clusters. After making sure that dad was engaged elsewhere, I approached the loudest reporter: a six-footer with city hair and a bad suit.

"They dinna' eat dog food."

The six-footer turned away from a bloke with a crucifix hanging around his neck on a blingy chain. "Cut! What?"

I looked back over his shoulder towards the cages. "They dinna' eat dog food. They've got dog heads, but they've got people bodies. They dinna' eat dog food. They eat food."

The six-footer lowered his mike and then his eyebrows. "You know them? You work here?"

I didn't drop my gaze, even though I wanted to. "Aye."

"You talk to them?" Those eyebrows nearly obscured the eager shine of his scrutiny.

I pretended to shrug. "Aye."

"Aye? 'Cause they won't talk to us."

I didn't answer him, and this had exactly the desired effect: he began backing me up towards the chicken wire, cutting me off from everyone else. "Twenty quid if you get us an interview." He flailed his too long arms around. "Billy! Get Cam one and a sound guy over here now. Fifty quid." He flashed a gold-toothed grin and I smelled night-before garlic. "Fucking a hundred, whatever you want, kid."

"I'll dae it for free."

Those eyes suddenly narrowed. "For free?"

I thought about it. For free would be weird, not to mention stupid. No dog-head had ever spoken out in public, I knew that (and I wasn't so certain that they would do now either), but I also remembered telling Vinnie that he should milk the bastards for all they were worth.

"A'right, for a care pack then – a fuckin' proper one. A stone ae beef: fillet and T-bone and rib-eye and ane ae 'em fancy-arse gas barbecues tae cook 'em on. Two twelve packs ae Peroni and a bottle ae good Laphroaig." I resisted looking at my numb feet. "And fuckin' marshmallows."

"Right." The suit looked less riled than I'd expected. "Anything else?"

I narrowed my eyes. "Some decent tobacco shag."

"That it?"

"Aye."

"Where?"

I elbowed my way free of the suit and the newly arrived cameraman and boom guy. "There." I pointed towards Cage Two.

~-oOOOo-~

Vinnie's dad saw us coming and got up out of his corner, elbowing aside an aggressive vanguard of his sons. He curled the ends of his fingers through the chicken wire. "Pete."

"You know this kid?"

"I do."

"Do you mind me asking how?"

"He's friends with my son."

I couldn't see Vinnie, but I knew he was there somewhere. I knew he was watching.

"Right." The six-footer looked a little bemused, but it didn't settle; he was far too twitchy with excitement. "Do you consent to an interview then? A proper one, no question out of bounds?"

Vinnie's dad glanced at me. His eyes were red-shot but dry. "I do."

The interview lasted a long time; the six-footer with city hair did his best to get his money's worth and then some, but Vinnie's dad was both patient and accommodating. The six-footer was too eager and too stupid to recognise a pattern in those questions that Vinnie's dad evaded. I was neither.

"So, would you say that you're happy here?"

Vinnie's dad blinked his dry eyes. "No. Would you be?"

The six-footer grinned, flashing gold again. "Would I be what?"

"Happy?"

The six-footer finally dropped his gaze, knocking his shoulder against mine before recovering his smarm. "I suppose not, no. But I'm not—"

"We're not asking to leave, we know that's impossible." Vinnie's dad swiped pale fingers across his nose and then folded his arms across his scarred chest. "We're just asking for the right to some freedoms, that's all. And maybe some respect."

The six-footer looked a little startled, and I had an idea that it wasn't down to Vinnie's dad's words or their solemn and assured delivery, but his own response to them. He caught my eye before he turned away from the cage and I saw it in his own.

Vinnie's dad pointed a finger at his jowly head and the cameraman kept rolling even as the six-footer walked away. "It's not this folk are afraid of." He looked briefly at me and showed his teeth before stabbing his finger into his scarred breastbone. "It's this."

The footage of Vinnie's dad circulated on the news and the internet for weeks. Some folks gave a shite, I'm sure, but most were more worried about the crashing markets, the protests, the freak weather, the price of fuel, and the scarcity of work and state sympathy. A few more reporters came down – a few gawpers too, if they coughed up enough – but Vinnie's dad didn't speak to any of them.

The evening after the interview, the dog-heads invited me to share their barbecue when I wandered past the Playground on my rounds. I guess it would've seemed a bit dicky not to ask me, but I was nevertheless chuffed to be beckoned over by one of Vinnie's scowling brothers, especially when Vinnie was nowhere to be seen.

I kneeled on the ground next to the chicken wire and accepted a half-drunk bottle of beer. It was cold. The brothers all squatted on their haunches, exposing their privates and looking at me. There were a lot of other dog-heads milling about or sitting in groups closer to the bracketed heaters. I didn't pay too much attention to them; in particular I'd made a careful habit out of not looking at the females – more out of embarrassment than courtesy, I suspect – though none of them looked my way either.

Vinnie's dad was standing next to the barbecue, but an old shaggy-headed dog-head was doing most of the cooking; the smoke billowed around his sagging skin like a grey halo. The smell was amazing. I couldn't remember ever having been at a barbecue before.

Vinnie's dad came over and passed a charred cut of beef through the fence. "Shared it out as much as we could, so there's not much left."

My mouth watered. "That's a'right. I've already eaten." Which wasn't true. "Where's Vinnie?"

Vinnie's dad showed his teeth as he sat down next to the fence. "Dicky tummy. Too used to dog food."

I didn't know how to respond to that, so didn't try. "You didna' tell the six-footer where ye were frae."

Vinnie's dad blinked his wet, yellow eyes at me. "No."

"Hey, mofo!" Vinnie bellowed, jogging over to the chicken wire and hitting it hard against his palm. His dad lowered his big head, pushing it close to Vinnie's teeth and snapping with his own.

"What? I'm learning the lingo. The TV's no good and Don Pedro here's a native."

I wasn't in any way responsible for *mofo*, but kept my mouth shut; I was far more intimidated by those sharp yellow teeth and the dark gums exposed by Vinnie's dad's rolled back lips than Vinnie was, despite there being a fence between us.

He squatted down opposite me. "Hey thanks for a' the shit–" he blinked, "shite."

"Shit," I corrected.

He grinned, tongue panting a little. "Shit."

"And it's cheers, no' thanks."

"Cheers."

I grinned, took a long swallow of the beer.

Vinnie's dad put his teeth away. "If you're so interested in knowing where we're from, son, you should get yourself down to a library, look us up," he said in a low voice. "You'll find us all over."

"Aye, or he could Google like a normal person," Vinnie said, embarrassed and something else – I couldn't tell what because I still struggled to read the dog-heads' expressions, but it was enough to make me feel bad again for ever asking.

"Who the hell's this?" The old, shaggy-haired dog-head had ambled over and now peered at me and my dad's gun, propped up against a fencepost.

Vinnie's dad seemed to relax a bit: his shoulders went down and he stopped looking at me so hard. "He's the son of one of the caretakers."

I stood up, and while I couldn't fit my whole hand through the chicken wire to shake, I tried to look like I wanted to. Since first meeting Vinnie, it had become very important to me that the dog-heads should like me, respect me – a ridiculous want, I can see that now, and one not without its own monstrous ego – they were like a family and family was what I craved. I thought more than freedom. I'm surprised Vinnie was never tempted to knock my block off.

"Hey. I'm Pete."

Shaggy-hair got the measure of me in one grey-eyed glance. "Yeah? Well you can call me fucking Rover."

A couple of the brothers laughed or growled, I couldn't tell which. "Wants to know where we're from," one of them said.

"Yeah?" Shaggy-hair grinned, but his eyes didn't blink. "You ever read a book, boy? We've been around since Ancient Greece. We've been Roman and Egyptian gods and Christian saints. Maps have us up mountains and down tunnels, dotted about Medieval Europe like a dose of the pox. Marco Polo found us in India, and the Chinese Empire followed us into Japan." He chuckled but it was without humour. I could smell his sweat; I could smell the sweat of the brothers behind him: stiff legged and tall, their ears erect and forward. They were all looking at me like I'd done something wrong. The only dog-head not staring at me was Vinnie; he was staring at the ground instead. "We even fought King Arthur's army in the hills of this city," Shaggy-hair growled, saliva dripping from the points of his teeth. "That enough for you, boy?"

"That's no' what I meant," I whispered, stepping away from the stink of the Playground as I did it.

"We Cynocephali wage war obstinately, drink human blood and quaff our own gore if we cannot reach the foe," Vinnie's dad said. I could see dark hairs rising along the silhouette of his shoulders.

I left then, saying nothing more and taking dad's gun and the empty bottle of beer with me. Vinnie didn't call me back, and I felt a sorrowful kind of fury: hurt that my fantasy of being part of any family had been so swiftly exposed and put down, and angry at the unjust nature of the exposure. But there was something else too. They had deliberately misunderstood me; their anger had been cruel because it had been a defence. As I trudged back towards Lindsay Road I nursed a growing suspicion alongside my hurt. I wondered whether any of the dog-heads did know where they'd come from. Or why they'd come back.

--o0O0o--

In the summer of that year, the caretakers' wages were cut again. People began queuing for food at Distribution Shelters set up inside bankrupted department stores. Temperatures rarely rose above those of spring and the rain never stopped; when I think back to that summer, all I can remember is a relentless symphony of drips and splashes and tinny chatter, choking drains and rushing rivers.

In August, dad had a massive heart attack while cleaning out the west side of the Playground. Vinnie told me later that dad had dropped like a stone; like all the life had been plucked out of the top of his head and into the murky clouds, leaving nothing behind but dead weight. He fell so hard that he smashed his nose and left cheekbone. His open eyes were studded with grit.

I was on the Walk, more than a mile away, when I heard the dog-heads howling. I expect that the whole north of the city heard that sound in their dreams for weeks: an endless, breathless gnarl of half alarm and half lament. Dad's cronies came running and found him face down on the concrete, while the dog-heads went on howling from behind the chicken-wire of every locked cage. One of the cronies, a monumental dick called Robert, was fond of telling anyone who'd buy him a drink that they'd felt like 'fuckin' gladiators in the fuckin' Colly-whatsit' as they'd dragged dad out amid the racket. The ambulance took more than an hour to turn up. Unfortunately, he still managed to make it.

Dad never forgave the dog-heads for saving his life. When he eventually came out of hospital, thinner and crankier than before, he returned to a very changed home: a son who had been making the most of his freedom, and a zoo that better resembled a recruitment agency. The first he put a swift stop to with his fury and wide-buckled belt, but there was nothing at all that he could do about the second. There was far more profit to be made in enterprise than in cruelty, and his old cronies now had new cronies.

They hired out the Beagles and Retrievers to an overworked and undermanned police force, ostensibly as sniffers and then bomb detectors. When the riots began to get more organised, the caretakers made bigger amounts bartering for the muscle of Bulldogs, Staffies and Mastiffs (Vinnie's brothers were popular). The women and the older ones were put to work in the flooded sewers in the vaults under South Bridge or keeping clean the big network of precious oil pipes along the north coast. Vinnie was mostly made to guard the latter; since the price hikes and strikes, lengthening power cuts meant that fuel depots, stations, and refineries were increasing targets.

I'd all but abandoned school by then, so most days I sat or patrolled the northern piers with Vinnie, chatting about everything and nothing as we looked out beyond the firth and the south bank, the only unspoken rule that the subject had to be present and existent; Vinnie wouldn't talk about the past and I didn't want to talk about the future.

--o0O0o--

That Christmas, we exchanged crap gifts within a few yards of the Albert Basin. Vinnie gave me a block of wood with the Hibernian badge carved into it – the only thing that looked vaguely like anything was the castle at its base. I gave him a battered old Ghost Rider comic book. Vinnie's dad and brothers sat around a drum fire some way off; another group of dog-heads hung around near the old mission. Much to dad's impotent fury, the dog-heads weren't locked up much anymore, although they went back to the cages to sleep willingly enough. The caretakers didn't exactly pay the dog-heads a fair swedge for their labour, but they were wise enough to see the gain in keeping them sweet with freedom, booze, and fags, and better food.

The night was cold, but for once not wet, though it might have been better if it had been. To the south, the sky above the city burned orange between pockets of black. Even so far away, the smoke was enough to water my eyes and burn the back of my throat. There was no longer much trouble in the north. When you're poor you don't much notice getting poorer; when you're already hungry, what's an extra rumble in your belly? My Christmas dinner had been out of date beans eaten cold from the can. Dad had made do with Special Brew. But those who'd always been the ones giving charity not taking it had found things a bit harder to accept. I was nearly not smug about that – mostly when I wasn't hungry.

"See her? Her–look!" Vinnie nudged me hard, nearly sending me sprawling.

"Whit? Who?"

"Her." Vinnie pointed out towards the group near the mission. "Her! Turn your light on."

I glanced down at dad's gun. I still carried it around with me; that was one of the few remaining rules. "I'm no' shinin' a fuckin' light on her like some perv in the bushes."

Vinnie grinned at me. "She's comin' over. Act fuckin' normal."

The dog-head looked different from most of them. She had a wild lion mane of pure white hair, a stubby snout and small triangular ears covered in brown fur. I was trying so hard not to look at her tits that I ended up ogling a lot worse.

Vinnie elbowed me hard in the belly. "Are ye lookin' at her fanny?"

"Naw! Fuck off, Vinnie."

Her laugh was scornful enough that I knew she'd heard. "Hey, Vinnie." She put her hands on her hips and didn't move. "You must be Pete."

I couldn't look at her, so I studied the barrel of dad's gun instead. "Aye."

"I'm Millie." She held out her hand.

I shook it quick and hard, and then let go. "Pleased tae meet ye."

She laughed again. "You sound like him."

I looked across at Vinnie and he was grinning wide, showing all of his teeth. "*He* sounds like *me*," I said, feeling bizarrely usurped.

She laughed again, and then turned away at another dog-head's shout. "See you later, guys."

Vinnie watched her walk away. I didn't. "You lot defo need clothes. It's fuckin' December. How come you're not all freezin' yer–" I caught a flash of Millie's arse before she disappeared into the shadows again and I stopped talking.

Vinnie ignored me. "I'm knockin' that."

"Hittin' that," I said, though I had a strong suspicion that he wasn't. Only a few of the dog-heads in the zoo had been either castrated or spayed; now that they'd become a workforce nobody cared. But I still had a strong suspicion that he wasn't.

"Aye," Vinnie grinned. "Whit that man said."

A whistle sounded inside the zoo and many of the dog-heads started moving off in its direction. Vinnie and I stayed put until Robert, the Monumental Dick and one of his sidekicks ambled over.

"On yer feet, pal," Robert said to Vinnie. "All hands on deck. Big fuckin' hooha on the Mile."

Vinnie's dad came over, the shaggy-haired dog-head behind. Since becoming an active member of the workforce he'd become known as Pipe Cleaner, so I'd resigned myself to never knowing what his real name had actually been.

"Aye, no' you two though, ken?" Robert scoffed. "About as much use tae me as yon Peter Pan o'er there."

"I'll be okay, Dad," Vinnie grinned, getting up. He punched me hard on the shoulder. In the light of the drum fire, his brown eyes shone black. "He's right, mofo, leave this tae the experts – ye wouldnae last five minutes among a' the irate suits and Sunday school teachers."

I grinned back in spite of myself as Vinnie swaggered off into the dark. "It's wouldna," I shouted. "Wouldnae's Weegie."

Pipe Cleaner peered at me like I was a big bug with wings. "What the fuck's he saying? That even a language?" He turned his gaze onto Vinnie's dad. "And they call us freaks."

Vinnie's dad didn't smile. "Give us a minute."

Pipe Cleaner left without a word, and pretty soon it was just me and Vinnie's dad and the roar of the far off North Sea and southern fires. I suddenly felt very sober.

"Why are you friends with my son, Pete?"

Vinnie's dad looked at me with those leaky, solemn eyes and nothing less than the truth seemed sensible. "'Cause he volunteered."

Something that might have passed for a smile exposed the points of his teeth. "You're a good boy."

I didn't answer. Over my shoulder, the wind picked up, rolling waves inland past the pier's tapered end.

"Some days I find myself wondering about people, Pete." He leaned close, and I could smell the cooked chicken on his breath though I could no longer see his eyes or the intent in them. "Do you think they'd behave the way they do if they thought someone was watching?"

I swallowed. "Ye mean like God?"

Vinnie's dad chuckled, but it wasn't a happy sound. "Why are you a good boy, Pete? Is it because you think you're being watched?"

He didn't wait for me to reply. He turned around and left, his bulk obscuring the drum fire before leaving its orange spit in his wake. I was glad, because I didn't know the answer – didn't understand the fucking question. Not then. But now I do wonder if I would have been the same person if not for Vinnie. I wonder what I might have become instead. Probably my dad. Most of all, I wonder about Vinnie's dad's question and the motive behind it. To the me then and the me now, it always sounded too much like a threat. One that ultimately ended up coming true.

--oO0Oo--

February the first of the following year was nearly the worst day of my life. It had plenty competition, but it beat all of them hands down. Until after.

Dad had already graduated from the ranks of drunk to jakie: he struggled to get off his arse even to piss. He smelled like something already half dead probably because he was. Booze hadn't dulled his mean streak though – it fed the only spark left in him. By then I was pretty much living in the mission, sharing a bunk with one of the new caretakers brought up from the city: a thick prick called Jaza. Dad came in one night and took his belt to us both, shrieking like a demented witch. After that I took to moving around, sleeping in different bunks, or with Vinnie and his family in Cage Two, or on an old mattress in the Playground, sometimes even on the harbour walls themselves, listening to the North Sea battering itself against concrete. Dad's old cronies might have been his cronies no longer, but they were scared shitless enough of him to leave well alone.

Pipe Cleaner found me out by the Martello Tower just as the sun began going down on the first. I'd been thinking of trying to cadge dinner off Vinnie's family when I saw him trying to run between the oil pipes, his hair whipped wild by the wind. When he stopped within ten yards of me, his hands drew into white fists and his eyes couldn't meet mine. They were wet.

"Is it Vinnie?"

Pipe Cleaner coughed, and then he sat down hard like someone had snipped his strings. I got up and sprinted back towards the zoo, but when I got there they'd already taken him away in a van. Vinnie's dad found me screaming nonsense at one of the brothers before wisely taking me off into the Playground to calm down.

Vinnie had been jumped coming back from a crowd control job in Restalrig. Half a dozen men had cut him off close to the dock office near the basin. Vinnie's dad's voice was as flat and inflectionless as always, but in my mind's eye, I could see how it had gone down only too well. Vinnie would have been too cool for fucking school at first, until he realised what was what. Then he would have tried to submit, because he wasn't an idiot: I'd seen him try to better his brothers. There was a bad picture in my head – that of Vinnie drawing back his lips and ears and dropping onto his knees, arching his back closer to the ground. Then he would have fought.

The wankers that found him took him to a vet. A fucking vet.

~-o0O0o-~

Vinnie didn't die. He came back less than a week later. He had a big comedy bandage wrapped around his head and his right leg was strapped up in an old-fashioned splint. His left arm hung limp inside a sling. I was only surprised that they hadn't given him one of those big cone things to stop him licking himself. The left hand side of his face no longer worked: his jowl drooped and his eye continually watered, unable to blink. While he'd been languishing inside what I've only ever been able to imagine as another much smaller Cage Two, Vinnie had suffered three strokes.

It was dad. They never said so – no one ever said so, fucking dad included – but I knew it was. And the fault in turn was mine because dad had hated Vinnie more than any other dog-head for no better reason than the fact that he'd been my only friend.

Vinnie didn't care. He greeted my tearful and wary first visit with the "fuck off, mofo!" that it probably deserved. His dad let me sleep on Vinnie's mattress on the floor of Cage Two for more than a week before making me return to the mission. I didn't go looking for dad. Some nights I sat at its old sash windows and watched the wash of light from the first floor of the first block of Lindsay Road flats until dawn, fantasising about the different ways I could kill him. All of them were slow.

~-o0O0o-~

As the riots in the city got worse, the dog-heads were permitted more and more freedoms. They were no longer locked up, not even at night, but as there was nowhere better for anyone to go – much less the dog-heads – it hardly mattered.

One day, on my way to visit Vinnie with a couple of tinnies that I'd stolen from the flat, after leaving some dog crap on the carpet next to dad's ugly snoring, I heard the unusual sounds of industry: hammers and drills and creaking ropes. Shouts, curses. Making a detour via the Playground, I stopped in amazement, fingers curling hard against the chicken wire.

The dog-heads were building. The buildings were wooden, but their footings were vast. My first thought was that they were chalet-like dormitories – some were already two floors high with piers reaching higher – but their walls were curved and shining with what looked like wax. For the first time, I felt apart from the dog-heads; even when Vinnie's dad recognised me and waved across the concrete expanse.

I found Vinnie sitting on a stool inside Cage Two, trying to flex his bad leg with a tin of spam tied to his ankle. He eyed me and the tinnies with equal relief.

"How's yer dad?" Vinnie had never voiced what we all knew either.

"Radge." I tried to grin. "But he'll get over it."

"Radgecase," Vinnie muttered, his ear pricking up when I finally managed to grin properly.

"Whit's yer dad and them doin' oot there?"

Vinnie rolled his good eye. "Reward for good service. The likes ae Robert, the Monumental Dick et al have finally let Dad and a' the rest ae them build their ane fuckin' hooses."

"Hooses?"

Vinnie blinked with his right eye, but couldn't quite catch either of mine. "Aye. Hooses. They're a' at it. Ye watched the TV lately?"

I shook my head. I didn't want to admit that I was too afraid to spend more than five minutes at a time in the Lindsay Road flat.

He gave me his lopsided grin. "All us dog-heads are buildin', buildin' – whit the fuck for my dad canna' explain. Thinks I'm still too delicate."

I snorted. "Ye are a wee flower."

"Fuck you."

"Naw, fuck *you*."

And then for a while that was it. The houses got finished at three storeys and then sat in polished state in the Playground, while the dog-heads mostly remained inside their cages or on the docks. In the cities, the rioting got worse, the weather got worse, the food and fuel shortages got worse. They'd begun talking openly about the end of the world by then.

When the power still worked, I sometimes watched online videos from elsewhere: juddering and pixelated footage of the same old story with different backdrops. For some, the Rapture had apparently been and gone while most of us had been paying attention to darker corners; now the Tribulation was underway. For everyone else there was only anger, confusion, fear, and a wonder at how this could be happening: a fiction only ever considered in abstract, in transitory guilt. Those of us in the zoo continued to enjoy the unlikely fortune of being spared less than the worst of it, and even drunken bigots like my dad knew it was only because of the dog-heads. For a time we were like a little ugly island cut off from the world. A sanctuary.

~-o0O0o-~

And then Vinnie disappeared.

His dad kicked me out of my bunk in the mission, his jowls shaking, eyes black.

"Vinnie?" I whispered, crouching on the floor.

We split up to search for him because I knew where he'd be. I waited until they'd all headed off in different directions – his dad, his brothers, Pipe Cleaner, Millie, all of the other dog-heads (because the caretakers wouldn't have given a flying fuck about a crippled freak, much less one that wasn't their own) – and then I snuck past the oil pipes and the Martello Tower before sprinting out towards the narrowing finger of the eastern dock.

The coastal wind grew and grew, pushing me back, shrieking old curses against my ears. My body nearly folding in on itself and my eyes streaming shut, I battled towards that red-flashing land buoy at its tip.

At first I couldn't see him (and was almost as relieved as I was disappointed), and then I glimpsed a shadow out towards the northeast end of the pier. When I eventually reached it, the shadow shuffled into a half-sitting position and spat into the wind.

"Fuck off, mofo."

"Vinnie, Christ." I hunkered down, grabbing hold of a wet post for balance. "C'mon, man, whit're ye doin'?"

He chuckled; I just about heard its rattling climax. I was more alarmed to see that both of his legs – good and bad – were already dangling over the edge.

"Vinnie!"

He turned his face towards me, its gold flashing alternate red. "It's alright, Pete."

I grabbed for his shoulder, but he flinched away, pulling his dead arm across his body.

"It's not fuckin' alright. What the fuck're ye doin'?"

"I'm nae use tae man nor beast." His right lip lifted, showing me his teeth. "I'm a jumbler."

"A jumbly," I corrected automatically. "And no ye're no' – c'mon, Vinnie. C'mon."

He looked out across the angry dark firth. "I never fucked her."

"Vinnie–"

"Will you make sure she's alright?"

I grabbed for him again, and when my fingers met his good arm he didn't flinch from their sharp pinch.

"It's not your fault, Pete."

He edged forwards, pulling his arm free of me. We could both hear the shouts far behind us in the wasteland, but all that remained real was that red-winking light on the edge of our world and our breath whipped away into black space.

Vinnie looked out into the churning firth and when he glanced back at me, I pretended not to see the terror in his eyes. "Listen to my Dad, okay?"

I didn't answer.

He punched my bicep hard enough to send shocks down through my numb fingers. "Fuckin' promise, mofo."

I nodded dumbly. My stomach swung like a dizzy lead weight. "Where are ye goin'?"

He gave a one-shouldered shrug, another lop-sided grin. "Burntisland, Kinghorn, Kirkcaldy, who the fuck knows?"

"Vinnie—"

"Fuckin' doggy paddle, eh?" And then he dropped from the harbour's edge like a stone. I think I screamed when I heard him hit the water. His chuckle came back at me, but I could tell that it cost him because it sounded completely alien – nothing like him at all. His shout was only a little more convincing. "See ya, Don Pedro!"

I kept watching him until the night beyond both the red-winking buoy and the moonlight hid his bobbing head from view. I tried to tell myself that he might make it to the opposite side of the firth – it wasn't so far: two miles if he swam the right way despite his bad arm and leg – but in the dark past what I could no longer see, I imagined Vinnie striking out towards the northeast, past the briefly reaching arms of Anstruther and North Berwick before being swallowed by the vast black cold of the North Sea. After that, I closed both my eyes and my mind.

~~o0Oo0~~

The rain came back and never stopped. Coastal areas quickly flooded, though the docks initially fared better than most. An Atlantic tsunami rolled across the Iberian Peninsula, reportedly wiping out both Portugal and Galicia and leaving the remainder of Spain and southern France under at least two feet of water. The rest of mainland Europe fared little better, and when reports stopped coming in from any other continent, I was nearly glad. The flood waters climbed slowly up from England. I remembered a long ago geography lesson about rising seas and tidal waters. Scotland was high enough above sea level that it could hold out longer than most. The Highlands were higher still. When coaches began lining up along the Walk, the caretakers, of course, managed to secure the choicest seats. Even dad roused himself from a drunken stupor long enough to pack an overnight bag.

The dog-heads refused to leave – not that they'd been offered the choice. Now they lived inside their shiny wooden *hooses* inside the

Playground, peering out onto the zoo and the wrecked city beyond through those little square windows. On the day that the buses were due to depart, I found Vinnie's dad inside the main doorway of the first one he'd help build. He watched me approach with his leaky and impassive yellow eyes.

"You off?"

I nodded. It was the first time he'd spoken a word to me since Vinnie had jumped into the firth.

He waited until I'd nearly made it as far as the empty cages before shouting my name. I stopped. Turned back. Walked back. The hard ground of the Playground muffled my return.

"Don't go," Vinnie's dad said. His large hands clenched into fists at his flanks.

I looked up at all the dog-head faces pressed up against those high, square windows.

Vinnie's dad blinked, his eyes narrowing, short ears pricked and head bowed. "Stay with us, Pete."

But in the end, I was too afraid.

--oOOo--

We barely made it into the mountains before the North Sea and the Atlantic swept over the central belt, crashing together in an unequal kiss that spilled back into the east, taking out Holland, Denmark and most of northern Germany. Before the internet winked out, I watched grainy CCTV footage of dog-head *hooses* across the world: in cities, on islands, and in the countryside. They were always the first to be swept away – before stone-built terraces and tenements, wooden sheds, even caravans – their waxy brown curves rolling deep against the icy black invading waters. I never knew if any of the ones I saw were from our zoo. I guess it hardly mattered.

--oOOo--

Now, we retreat higher and higher, moving around like nomads. There's no power, little food. Little land. If you believe the ranting zeal of converts like my dad, we've another four and a half years to wait before God comes back to get us. There's a group of nutters a few miles up the road who've got some Jewish book that says when the Messiah returns 'the face of the generation will have the face of a dog'. Crap like that's enough for most folk now. Just about everything's enough for most folk now: a full moon; the shiver of someone walking over their grave; looking at the wrong person the wrong way at the wrong time. Life's become pretty academic.

Not a day goes by that I don't regret breaking my promise to Vinnie. In my dreams, I imagine saying yes to his dad; I imagine disappearing inside the cool brown gloom of his wooden hoose and standing alongside him and Pipe Cleaner and Millie and the Bulldog brothers as we're borne away by the angry oceans.

I would have been less afraid then than I am now – even before I understood what I'd been offered. But I earned my place and then squandered it. And that's only down to me. On cold, lonely nights when that knowledge becomes almost too hard to bear, I think of Vinnie shouting "See ya, Don Pedro!" as he struck out into the dark abyss beyond the firth. My belly grows heavy and my chest warm. And I no longer feel alone.

Carole Johnstone's short stories have appeared in numerous magazines and anthologies. She has been published by PS Publishing, ChiZine Publications, Night Shade Books, TTA Press, Apex Book Company, and Morrigan Books among many others. Her work has been reprinted in Ellen Datlow's Best Horror of the Year *series and Salt Publishing's* Best British Fantasy 2013 *and* 2014.

EXTRA BODY PARTS
by Justin Grimbol

I was checking on a patient's blood pressure, when I noticed a scar. It was on his left hand. The client told me it was from an extra finger. This was a drug rehab. Many of the clients had scars and weird growths and cysts. But I had a feeling this extra finger wasn't from drug use.

"I was born with tons of extra body part," he said. He showed me his extra nipples and the scar where his extra toes used to be. His toes were webbed. "I used to have three dicks," he said. "But I got one of them removed."

"You have two dicks? Do they both work?"

"Of course. One's bigger than the other, but they both get hard. They both squirt."

I was amazed. As techs, we were supposed to keep our client's information confidential, but I couldn't keep this a secret. I told everyone about the man with two dicks. Meeting someone with two dicks just seemed so incredible. The world felt full of magic again. It was like meeting a unicorn or a dragon, or a dragon-shark, or fairy with three big tits.

My friend Carl was not impressed.

"Would you even want two dicks?" he asked.

"What kind of question is that?" I said. "Of course I would want two dicks."

"I think it would be awkward. How would you manage it?"

"You put one in the poon and one in the anus. This isn't rocket science."

"What if she doesn't want it in the butt?"

"Then you shove both in the normal spot. Or you let one dangle, no big deal."

"I guess."

We were at the Godfather's book store, sitting at the coffee bar. A homeless man sat at the other end of the shop with his big motorcycle helmet on his head. We called him Helmet 'cause he always wore that thing on his head. The guy heard everything we said. All our dick talk. He started laughing and mumbling. I think he said something about his dick. I raised my cup to him.

"Here's to you good sir," I said. "I'm sure you have a thick powerful sabre."

Helmet laughed and mumbled about random stuff.

"I don't know why you hang out in here," Carl said. "It's so sketchy. This bookstore is sleazier than most dive bars."

"I like it's that way," I said. "I think it's fun."

My friend Chris, who lived in the basement of the book store, came up and sat with us. I told him about my double dicked friend.

He smiled. "That's so cool," he said.

"Here's to having two dicks," I said.

We raised our coffee mugs.

Helmet laughed.

~~o0O0o~~

I worked with a woman named Loni on Sundays. She was skeptical about the client having two dicks. We needed verification. But how could we get it without seeming unprofessional?

We called the client into the med room.

"Listen dude, I know this is really unprofessional and even a little creepy," I said. "But I got to see the double dick. I got to see it. It's the only way I can know it's real."

Loni nodded. "I got to see it too."

The client laughed. "I don't actually have two dicks," he said. "I was just fucking with you."

The three of us laughed hysterically. I was glad he didn't get offended by me asking to see his dick. That was not very professional of me. We had a good laugh over it. We laughed hard.

It was funny. But the client noticed that, even though I was laughing, I looked sad. I was really sad that he didn't have two dicks.

He gave me a hug, which, I'm pretty sure, we weren't supposed to do. Hugging clients was not professional. We were breaking a lot of boundaries that day.

Justin Grimbol was raised by chubby ministers in Sag Harbor, New York. He moves around a lot. At the moment he lives in Oneonta New York with his wife, Heather. He spends his time flirting with her, hiking and feeling scrappy. He is the author of Drinking Until Morning, The Creek, The Crud Masters, The Party Lords, Naked Friends, *and* Hard Bodies.

SEXUALITY & INNOCENCE
by Kirk Jones

Author Chimamanda Ngozi Adichie was recently quoted on Upworthy.com saying, "We teach girls shame. Close your legs, cover yourself. We make them feel as though being born female they're already guilty of something." The phenomenon Adichie discusses—imposing sexuality on the image of the human body—has become such an integral part of societal regulation that we barely give it a second thought. And teaching girls shame is only the tip of the iceberg. For many, anxieties about sexuality lead us to suppress anything that might carry with it connotations of sex. We cover our bodies in fear that it might elicit some threatening response. Sadly, we live in a world where such reactions are often justified. When pro-rape rhetoric claims entitlement to the bodies of others, who wouldn't be anxious about revealing their body? How could we view the body as anything other than sexual when we think about our safety? Finally, who wouldn't want to protect the innocent from potential victimization later in life?

Despite the motivation, the desire to control and suppress sexuality through covering it and hiding it has become so strong, we have acquired the impulse to suppress gestures with sexual connotations before females even reach sexual maturity, as Adichie discussed. We read into behaviors, using our anxieties as a dowsing rod to identify potentially "dirty" acts and correct the young if they exhibit any curiosity about the human body. Sadly, the escalation of these anxieties to titanic proportions isn't far from their depiction in John Waters' *Desperate Living*. When Peggy Gravel sees her children naked, she runs from the room, screaming to her husband in the neighboring room, "The children are having sex. Beth is pregnant!" She's imposed her anxieties and fears about sexuality onto her children, who aren't even biologically capable of doing or being any of the things she accuses them of. As she beats her children for this indiscretion, it becomes obvious that the corrective measure she employs serves more to squelch her anxiety than properly raise her children. If nothing else, the understanding of one's body as dirty or wrong has been transmitted through the corrective action.

Sadly the scene is only a slightly dramatized reflection of what happens in our society today. We've been conditioned to see the exposed human body as dirty or wrong. In turn, we see our own bodies as a source of filth or shame. Gymnophobia, the fear of being naked, is now a commonplace anxiety . . . and we share all of these values with the next generation.

Oddly enough, at the same time these sexual anxieties reach a crescendo in our culture, and we work to suppress any inkling of sexuality that the body exhibits, cartoons and puppet shows emerge that infuse images associated with childlike innocence with sexuality.

And the ratings soar.

What the fuck? When anxieties about sexuality are so high in our society that we've infused the innocent with a sense of shame to protect them from very potential threats, why would viewers gravitate towards shows that infuse depictions of innocence with sexuality? While it seems contradictory at first glance, there are contexts in which it makes sense.

Infusing signifiers of childhood and innocence like puppets and cartoons with sex is by no means a recent trend. Initially, animation was conceived as a form of entertainment for adult audiences. Even when the animation featured bubbly, wide-eyed characters, many early cartoons dealt with adult themes and featured coarse language. It took decades before animation became characterized by its newfound demographic: children. Of course, even then adult themes still cropped up in cartoons, whether via subliminal flashes like the topless woman in Disney's *The Rescuers*, or craftily veiled sexual innuendo, such as those that slipped through the censors in the early works of John K and Ralph Bakshi's *Mighty Mouse: The New Adventures*. But artists like John K have acknowledged that most of what they did could be attributed to disgruntled cartoonists having little creative input, a ubiquitous "fuck you" to the animation groups that hired them and threw shitty scripts into their studios on a weekly basis. And these flashes of sexuality didn't function as the primary focus in the show.

For the most part, adult cartoons stayed off the airwaves until a few decades ago, around the early 90s. Some of the first successful examples came not long thereafter, including *Family Guy*, a handful of shows featured on Cartoon Network, and *South Park*.

To this day, *South Park* remains one of the most popular television shows on air. Just about everybody loves it. I love it. Part of the appeal of *South Park* is watching these cute little cartoon characters open their mouths and listening to the curse words accumulate. It was the very seeming contradiction of cutesy, crudely drawn characters spitting out curse words that perhaps took us back to our days of drawing stick figures fucking, at least that's what it did for me. And perhaps that's what infusing the innocent cartoon characters with forbidden adult privileges of drinking, taking drugs and cursing is all about. The cursing and sexuality hearkens back to a time when we longed to be adults. At the same time, the cartoon elements cater to our desire as adults to be young and care free again.

Since *South Park* hit the airwaves in 1997, adult cartoons have become the norm on network television. And just like any trend, the media has a propensity towards upping the ante. Just like horror films have gravitated towards increasing the amount of gore, televised animation encroaches upon the boundaries of innocence to elicit a response and generate controversy.

The result of upping the ante is best encapsulated by this trend's most accurate parody, *Sex Puppets*, featured in Warren Ellis' *Transmetropolitain*. After watching MTV's *Wonder Showzen*, which aired in 2005, you'd have to wonder if the creators took cue directly from Ellis' *Sex Puppets*. The soft pornographic depictions of brightly-colored, wide-eyed puppets masturbating are so removed from actual sex that they're a far cry from causing arousal. If anything, the seemingly paradoxical mixture of signifiers of innocence with sex is extremely unsettling. It is no surprise the show was not a success. Still, you have to wonder why it aired in the first place. Is the sexualization of innocence in cartoons and puppet shows some sort of reptilian-illuminati media conglomerate means to reinforcing the sexual anxieties in our society, as a few of my friends and acquaintances might suggest? Or perhaps the sexualization of innocence in cartoons is a means to rebelling against sexual anxieties in our culture. If the latter of these two options is the case, there is a threshold at which rebelling against sexual anxieties fails. That threshold is reached when the signifiers of innocence are so pronounced that the references to sexuality disturb us as adults rather than hearkening back to our own childhoods before our anxieties arose.

So what are these signifiers of innocence? Think Precious Moments dolls as the highest echelon: large, bulbous eyes, button noses, bright and/or lightly hued colors associated with childhood. The stumbles and staggers of toddlers, i.e. awkward movement, the dialect of youth, including improper pronunciation and arrangement of words, toys, and ignorance. *Wonder Showzen* used all of these in their show, coupling each of these signifiers with depictions of masturbation, sex, menstruation, phallic imagery, and more.

Shows like this, along with countless others, seem to tap into our fears and anxieties related to sexuality. As the entertainment industry continues to up the ante, there's bound to be more material like this in the future. So what do we do about it? I'm no advocate of censorship, which is why I think raising awareness about the effects the media has on us is an important way to curb some of the troubling trends in our society. If we're ever going to get back to a place where we can be comfortable with ourselves, to a time before we ate the shame-inducing apple that was pushed upon us by serpent-like biblical passages of long ago, and the cultural values reinforced by the media, we need to take a long, hard look at ourselves in the mirror—preferably naked—and realize that shame and doubt, just like sexuality, is something we impose upon the image of the body, and the way we read our bodies both in social contexts and in isolation is something we have control over, not something that needs to succumb to the whims of neuroses.

Kirk Jones *entered the bizarro scene as part of the New Bizarro Author Series in 2010. Since then, he has had work published by Lazy Fascist Press and Omnium Gatherum. His second book,* Journey to Abortosphere, *was published in 2014. He is currently an acquisitions editor for Rooster Republic Press.*

QUICK AND EASY
by Michael Sean LeSueur

Stop. It's nothing, go. Push the cart down the street. Toss your dripping gloves in. Ditch the saw. Dump the rancid bags in the can. Light a cigarette. Smoke it out. It's always the same; butchered flesh, a tedious job. Lights flash. A window rolls down; payment for services. Now, to spend your evening... You flip a coin: heads. Time to stop for a drink. An old-fashioned, with fashionable company. You cross the street; heel a puddle. You pat down your dress: clean cotton. You tear off the soaked and clinging hose. Saved by the peel.

You step into the bar. Take in the atmosphere. Drowned sorrow and unrequited lust abound. At the end of the bar, look: Blue eyes. Slick black hair. Grey tailored suit. C'mon, Heather. It's your move. King at E-5, Queen to C-5. Quick-take at the prize. He's game. You light up. A drink slides over: White Russian. Not your usual, but you take it. You sip and he slips close. Daniel's his name. Accounting. In the running to take over his wife's company. Likes red-heads. You appreciate his good taste. You do freelance journalism, but tonight... It doesn't matter.

You get him back to your studio. Quaint place. Came cheap, too. You pour yourself the old-fashioned of olde yearn-ed. He slinks up behind and explores your skin-matte with a finger along your spine. You smirk and rub against him. Run your fingers through his hair. You turn around, bare twin mattress behind him, and you push him to bed. You empty the glass; follow in for suit.

He likes women who take charge. Submissive men: you know their kicks. You take off his belt. Wrap it around your fist. Nibble the buckle. You tear his shirt open; buttons fly. He has plenty more in the closet. You bring the belt to his neck. He smirks. Right. On. Tighten it. You undo his trousers. Stroke and strain, loving in the pain. Blue and flush in the face. He doesn't last long.

You giggle and spark one up. Give him a few. He'll be good again, so take more time than he needs. Stare at the ceiling. You finish your pack. You take some of his. His wife's been sneaking around. While he's working for her, no less. Something you can relate to.

Her name's Helena: Brunette. Always wears yellow. She sees Rob every day at 6 when she comes home just in time for dinner.

Rob: a senior executive manager for IBM. A big wig. Kruther's is their haunt. 42nd street.

It hurts Daniel. You take pity and offer *special services.* Do whatever you have to. Make her pay. You kiss. A cig later, and he passes out.

The next day: you purchase another saw, pack some gloves, and head out to Kruther's at 5:30. It's kitschy and sedate for the most part, but the reuben's good. A few couples have an early dinner. Suits lounge at the bar: nothing exciting.

A canary walks in late at 6:15. She calls out to the bar. The man in the middle greets her. She orders a screw-driver. He nurses straight whiskey. They down them over sensual chatter. They're geared up to go at it. You follow them to a cheap inn. You nurse lobby-coffee in front. Helena comes out some thirty minutes later. You don't stay long enough to see Rob.

Helena struts down the block. She calls a cab. You snatch her purse. She chases you. You lead her down an alley. You hide behind an old box, and Helena stands there looking around. You chloroform the skank. She falls, and you get to work. You bag up the bits, stuff them in the box, and the neighborhood cat's meow and claw at the offal mess. Let them have it; the job's done.

You head back to your place. Daniel's still asleep, so you take a shower. Wash down dried blood. You snuggle up to Daniel. Your fresh hair tickles his nose. He moans and looks up at you. Slanted, hung-over eyes: so adorable. Everything's taken care of, you tell him. He checks his schedule: the next few days are off. His phone vibrates. You toss it out the window: he needed a new one soon. A door slams down the hall. You smile and undo his trousers: a welcome break before the next job. After all, they're never this quick and easy.

Michael Sean LeSueur is an actor, singer, and author who resides in Scottsdale, Arizona. They specialize in bizarro, horror, scifi, and crime. You may remember them from such strange films as Cavemen on a Train *and* Space Monkeys on Ice. *Michael is the author of* Pixiegate Madoka *from Eraserhead Press' New Bizarro Author Series. Their hobbies include watching films, taking photos of abandoned locations, and eating sushi. Their work can be seen in* Fifty Secret Tales Of The Whispering Gash: Queefrotica.

Find them on:
Facebook: www.facebook.com/FilmAddict.MichaelSeanLeSueur
Instagram: instagram.com/msuspiriorum/
    (or search for msuspiriorum)
Twitter: https://twitter.com/msuspiriorum

FROM COLLEAGUE TO COLLAR
by Sauda Namir

All my life, I've been the type people come to for sex conversation. Not just friends, but barely acquaintances. Not just advice, but permission to explore their own sexuality. I live in the gray areas, dabbling in extremes with enthusiastic curiosity. I'm a polyamorous, sapiosexual, switch; a feminist, nude model, and burlesque artist. It may be coded in my pheromones, this universal understanding that I won't judge you for paraphilias. It doesn't matter the topic: physiological or psychological, personal or societal, practical or fantasy. I'm a safe place to air your views and examine your reflection. I embrace this phenomena, and encourage those around me to live sexually. There is an element of sex in everything, and anything can be sex.

Fuck your friends. I say it so often, it is practically a catch phrase. That doesn't mean I want to smash my clit against everyone I know. You see, I'm an incurable flirt. I don't put people into neat little boxes which are labeled to the exclusion of all others. I let them roam around the vast and intricate venn diagram of intimacy, however we mutually see fit. When I first laid eyes on Michael, he was performing in Hot & Heavy Burlesque's Tribute to Pink Floyd's *The Wall*. I was attracted to him, but pretty oblivious to any infatuation he might have been harboring. He was a colleague, a fellow performer, and therefore a new friend. I'd felt that immediate affinity before, it is what happens when two open books meet.

Fast forward to a Tuesday night on the west side more than a year later. I'm at a munch for local kinksters, and who should walk in but this friendly face I met in the burlesque scene. I rush over to say hello, and sit in his lap. (Flagrantly ignoring the stringent rules of public contact at the munch.) That night, I knew we shared more than a love of performance. We were nerds for games, cats, and music. As soon as I lurked his FetLife profile, I knew we were compatible in an untold number of ways. Soon, to my delight, we started skipping munches in favor of private discussions over dinner and drinks. The more I learned about him, his past, his experiences, the more addicted to time with him I became. Quickly, gazing into his ecstasy over carrot cake waffles became erotic. We were having foodgasms together long before orgasms. All the same, it was intensely pleasurable. Oxytocin levels soared; we were having great sex with the largest sexual organs - our minds.

An immense amount of credit must go to Michael for taking a leap of faith on me. He was the first to verbalize everything he wanted. So many people live in a tower, built around them block by block with fear. Fear of rejection, fear of misunderstanding, a fear that sharing the truth will ruin that which we have. He knew he had nothing to lose. Whatever we might become, we were not going to end our friendship. After acknowledging what our affections had already chosen, we agreed to formalize our relationship as BDSM play partners. It was a short-lived plan. The truth was we were lovers. At the intersection of kink and companionship, there is a place where a runaway train of emotions can carry you off. I let it. Never have I forged such an instant connection with a partner as the one I hold now.

Over the course of our relationship, no intimacy has been held back. We are more than "safe, sane, consensual" - we are in constant communication of our most vulnerable lust. The depth of trust and honesty we share has given me the most extravagant sex of my life. We're both incredibly GGG (good, giving, and game). No fantasy is too much to share. We still have and respect our hard limits, but talking about them is always on the table. When we listen to each other, we validate those thirsts. No awkward shame exists between us; nothing that must remain hidden to protect our fragile egos. In more than one instance, these tête-à-tête have made me examine my own limits, work past inhibitions, and revise my opinions to have spectacular firsts!

While I identify as a switch, I am blissfully submissive to Michael. Formal negotiation of a scene is crucial when the tryst is designed to satisfy a very specific craving, or when entering the territory of darkest desires. I have a strong taste for sensual depravity; consensual non-consent being an exceptional thrill. More often, we're faced with a complete embarrassment of riches, allowing our play to meander in whichever direction impulse drags us. His ability to take me over is almost orgasmic in and of itself. Some time ago, I was compelled to describe the natural high of falling into subspace:

> Come together, time falls apart
> Touch ignites delirium
> Pin me down, I soar infinitely higher
> Strike inspires passion
> Inflict your stinging pain, an intense pleasure remains
> Command impresses faith
> Regardless of tangible bind, control my form and mind
> Lust imbues trembling
> Violate my every plane, teach me to feel fully alive
> Only then may I thrive

When I enter this mindset, I'm thoroughly entranced. I refer to it as "going under" since the feeling is of a serene drowning. Every moment is sheer euphoria, and I'm at the complete mercy of my partner. One of my cues is falling silent, practically non-verbal on my own accord. I'll repeat phrases, but am unlikely to offer anything new. Sensations of pain may be dulled, but sensitivity is at an all time high. The slightest variant in any series of touch can send me scrambling. For as much as I enjoy spanking, electrosex, and bondage... it is always the psychological element which gets me there. The ritual of kneeling for my collar is practically Pavlovian. From there, a barrage of delicious indignities will send me. Demands for domestic servitude, preferably performed roughly exposed, and subjected to sugarcoated derision; that's where I begin to melt. Sex of any stripe - including the harsh and humbling - is boundlessly gratifying when mutually given fervently, accepted graciously, secure in radical emotional exposure, and with faith in the bonds of passion.

__Sauda Namir__ is a multifaceted artist with a penchant for titillation. She's a burlesque artist, nude model and photographer for both Zivity and GodsGirls, thriller actress, and bisexual, poly, kinky, sexpositive visionary. Sauda lives in Chicago with her incurably supportive partner and a very fun cat. You're cordially invited to get all the intimate details on her website, SaudaNamir.com.

DEEP DRAW
by Neil Williamson

"Say, son. Do you want to hear a story?"

Fat fingers tugged the sleeve of my shirt. Under its Angelino camouflage, the old fellow's face was *brimming*.

Did I want to hear a story? As if the timing of me coming by his table was a coincidence.

The tropical storm raged against the windows. Reflected in the streaming glass, the airport hotel bar was all but empty. Just a few desultory sots spending an unplanned evening away from home. Sitting in their self-absorption, stirring who knew what stories. I could have chosen any one of them to tap, but this old West Coaster was ready to spill. It was obvious from the second he walked in, grumbling about the flight cancellations, complaining that people didn't get treated like this in LA. A stream of babble directed at no one in particular until he found his way to the bar and asked for a whisky. *One of the good ones.* By which he meant a conspicuously expensive scotch, but I've been a barman a long time: when a customer demands a drink you don't give him the one he asks for, you give him the one he needs.

For the sake of appearances, I hovered, rubbed at an imagined speck on the mouth of the water carafe I happened to be holding.

"If the manager catches me slacking off—"

His eyes crinkled. "You're not worried about your *manager*."

"No." I placed the empty carafe on the table, sitting it just so behind the bright distraction of the candle glass. "No, I'm not."

"My name is Vincent Deluca," he said once I was seated and he had my full attention. "I'm a Hollywood man."

He wanted me to be impressed. I've served water, in all its forms, everywhere from the banks of the Ganges to the highest table on Olympus. And even Olympus struggled to match Hollywood for misplaced self-importance. This introduction wasn't a pleasantry, it was an establishment of our dynamic; high to low. And that suited me fine.

True to form, Deluca didn't offer to shake my hand. Neither did he ask my name. I could have told him: *Ganymede*. But to do so would have changed the gradient between us before the flow had even started. So, instead, I replied with an indulgent smile.

"Forty five years in the movie business," he said. "You know what it takes to last that long in Hollywood?"

I refrained from rolling my eyes. He really wanted to bang the *Hollywood man* thing home. The cinema is a useful tool, but not one I hold in much regard. At its best it is capable of piquancy that almost echoes truth, but at its worst, like chick-lit novels and soap operas and sci-fi shows and *bandes desinée*, it generalises and dilutes. In my experience, the majority of Hollywood men treated story like a cheap currency, squandering it disdainfully.

The only tales of value are true ones. Those treasured by the gods are unique. They are seldom spoken, and to obtain them takes skill.

"Oh," I said lightly. "I'd imagine: pluck, luck, and a ruthless streak that'd make Chuck Bronson look like Little Orphan Annie."

He liked that, gave me an appraising look that took in the ambrosia blond of my tied-back hair, the sandstone stubble on my chiselled chin, the old Adriatic eyes. He leered like a man half his age. I didn't react to that, kept my expression friendly but neutral. He'd promised me a story. I wanted him to focus on it.

"Damn fucking right you do." He said it *sotto voce* into his glass, sipped, then took a moment to appreciate the scotch blossoming in his mouth. It made him cough; a dry, indelicate hack. He wiped his lips on a napkin.

"So, this story." He was ready at last. But first, another look, a different kind of appraisal. "I guess you're not old enough to remember Sandie Laurence? She was an actor, early-to-mid seventies—"

"Sure, I've heard of her," I lied. I didn't want to be here all night. "YouTube, yeah?"

Deluca grunted. "Well, then you know Sandie." He relaxed in his chair. "Terrible actress. Terrible. *Abysmal*. But talent is overrated.

She was a looker, and she had one skill: she could cry. Jesus, could she cry. So, she had a career. Started off in the soaps and cop shows, moved up to TVMs. Frightened hooker in *Ironside*, aggrieved widow in *Columbo*. You'd know her face for sure. It'd be the one with tear-tracks through her make-up. Anyway, her modest skills earned her a studio contract, and she starred in a string of moderately successful weepies. She even made the long list for Love Story before they gave the part to Ali. You get the picture. Anyway, at some point she started to believe she *was* something, and then she started to behave like it too. We're not talking Lyndsey Lohan, but throwing trailer fits, holding up production, demanding changes in the script. Pain in the fuckin' ass. You know what I'm saying?"

As I nodded, I glanced at the carafe. The glass had begun to mist inside. It might have been caused by proximity to the heat of the candle, but it wasn't. "Directors stopped wanting to work with her?"

He snorted. "Damn fucking right. But around about the time she started acting up she also raised her game. Those tear-jerkers started getting respectable box office. There was even a whisper of an Academy Award nomination. So, the studios wanted her. For a while."

"Until?"

"Until her last film. Another trashy piece of emotional blackmail. We're talking doomed relationship, terminally ill child, and a whole load of that love-and-peace shit. Well, it was the seventies. Picture was called Franco's Wish. Had a budget too; Martin Schiller directed, 2nd unit location filming in Spain for the *dego* scenes. Shit as the script was, that movie could have made her. Instead it finished her."

Deluca rolled his glass again. Shark-grinned into it as he sipped, savoured, stretched out the moment. Just a hint of a cough as he drank it down. He was hitting his stride now.

"So this was, let me see, spring seventy three? I was still new to the business, but I'd got myself a job as an assistant to a producer named Harold Gravey. That was really his name. For a while the girls in the office tried to stick me with the nickname, *Biscuits*, because I was always tagging around after him. But fuck that, right?

It didn't even work. Anyway, what assistant meant—taking calls, running errands, driving people from airports to hotels to studios. Yada, yada. And on the location shoot for Franco's Wish, I was the kid who got to run around after Sandie Lauerence. And, man, she was hard work." He put on a voice, thin and screechy. "Vincent? Vincent! Come here now."

His impression sounded exactly like Bette Davis calling for her sister in *Whatever Happened To Baby Jane*. Like he couldn't remember the difference between memory and the movies. Or maybe he just thought it sounded more dramatic. The false note irked me. It diluted the truth so prized by my customers.

"So, one day we're shooting exteriors in a vineyard up in the hills off the 101. It's one of her big scenes and the director's setting up for a sunset shoot. I'm sent to get her from her trailer to run through the scene, and she tells me: 'Tell that man', that was what she called Schiller, *that man*. 'Tell that man I don't want to do this scene today.' Now I know what Schiller will say. He'll hit the fucking roof to hear this now. Once the sun starts to set we've got maybe a thirty minute window before we lose the light. But I trot off dutifully and tell him. And then he comes to her trailer and they have words, and when he's gone she calls me in and says: 'You've got to get me to a telephone'. Like that. Wide-eyed and deadly serious. Like she's in one of her crappy pictures."

Deluca spread his hands. "What am I to do? I'm eighteen years old, but I do happen to know there's a house close by. The people that run the winery, right? I sneak her over there in the studio car and she turns on the movie star eyes and, of course, she gets her phone call. Fifteen minutes later we're back in her trailer. It's starting to get dark. Schiller's been over twice and Sandie's promised she'd be there shortly, but that she's not ready. Not yet. So we sit."

Deluca laughed dryly. "At least I sit. Not Sandie. But she's not prepping for the scene, she's not using the method, she's not doing mantras or any of that calming, holistic shit. She's pacing and she's smoking like a three alarm fire, and every two minutes she peeks through the curtain. And she's making me nervous too. I mean, I'm just a kid, right? I'm shitting bricks thinking I'm about to have to

196

deal with a highly paid movie star's full blown nervous collapse, you know?

"Then there's a knock at the door, and Sandie composes herself. 'Let her in and wait outside,' she says. I open the door to an extremely unhappy young woman. I just stand there like a sap, trying to work out how a woman dressed for working on the farm—there are sawdust sprays on her blue jeans, oil stains on her plaid shirt—and in an obvious fucking rage can possibly look this beautiful. The object of my absorption, of course, doesn't even see me, just pushes past me to confront Sandie. I'm smart enough not to hang around, but before the door closes I see the visitor dump a grocery sack on the table, and say: 'You can't keep on doing this.'

"Whatever passes between them doesn't take long. Sandie's visitor soon storms out of the trailer again and takes off in a muddy Dodge truck. And *poof!* Sandie appears at the trailer door and announces she's ready. Anyway, long story short, right? They shoot the scene and catch the sunset and she's stunning in it. Stunning. The perfect combination of melodrama and real emotion. How she managed to bring those marshmallow lines to anything approaching life is a miracle. But she did. Exactly what the director's looking for. Everyone goes home happy, right?

"Hey what are you doing? Are you even listening to this?"

I'd only diverted my attention from the great impresario for a second. Just long enough to check the carafe again, satisfy myself with the drips streaming down the inside of the glass. "Course I am." I smiled reassurance. "Everyone's happy. Right."

"Wrong, wise ass." Deluca pulled a face and I thought for a second I'd blown it, but the rain, the whisky, an audience... The story was flowing too well now.

"Sandie wasn't happy at all. She was a wreck. Everyone could see how much the performance took out of her. Possibly even earned herself some respect among the crew. I knew there was more to it, of course but had no idea what, and Sandie wasn't in the mood for sharing.

"Well, the rest of the shoot was in the studio in Burbank, and everything returned to normal pretty fast. Sandie reverted to being a bitch and the crew to being frustrated. She never once mentioned what happened in the vineyard, and it wasn't my place to ask. I was just there to deal with her shit.

"Of course, it happened again. She'd been putting off the scene where the husband leaves her. Kept begging Schiller to postpone it until later in the schedule; which he did, bending over backwards to oblige her until they couldn't delay it any longer.

"So, same routine: Sandie confines herself to barracks and won't come out for anyone. Outside her locked dressing room door we can hear her going through her lines, trying a hundred ways to say the same words. Then, for almost a whole day, there's silence, until finally she comes out and once again she summons the visitor.

"'Where's the fucking bitch this time?' When I meet the young woman at the studio gatehouse, she's no less beautiful and maybe twice as angry. I escort her to Sandie's dressing room and they have a real screaming match in there, but I'm fucked if I can make out any details. I'm thinking the visitor is her supplier, of course, but people in that line of work are seldom so reluctant to deliver. Unless Sandie wasn't paying her bills, but then you turn up with a thirty-eight and guy named Angelo, don't you? Anyway, when the visitor leaves and Sandie toddles off at last to do the scene, I search the dressing room but the only thing that wasn't there before is a grocery bag with a Goody's soda bottle in it. And there's nothing more suspicious in that than a dribble of water.

"So, Sandie does the scene. Unbelievable. Nails it first take. The actor playing the husband barely keeps it together. Everyone's in tears. Even me."

"All from a little water?"

That made Deluca laugh so hard he started to cough again. He shook his head, red faced.

"Are you all right?"

"I'm fine," he choked. "Fine. Just a little inoperable cancer."

"That doesn't sound *fine*."

He wiped his lips on his napkin again. "Son, I've got the best doctors in the world. I pay them to tell me it's fine. You understand?"

While he gathered himself I glanced at the carafe again. The water that hadn't been there before. Then I asked: "And the third time?"

"How'd you know there was a third time?"

"There's always a third time in stories."

Deluca's nod acknowledged that. "Heh, well, it's the last day of the shoot. There's a mixture of relief and apprehension on set. Everyone's glad the beast is almost in the bag. They know it's not Oscar material, not even with Sandie's waterworks, but it's just about getting it wrapped now. And she still has the final scene to shoot. The one where the kid dies. Oh, hey, really that's not a spoiler if you ever watch it. It's pretty much obvious from the opening titles, I promise you.

"Anyway, same routine. Come the big moment, Sandie delays. Everyone has a go at getting her on set. If Schiller had any hair he'd have been tearing out by the roots. Eventually, I go to her: 'Sandie, this happens every time. Just call her and get it over with.'

"Her face is like stone. 'Vincent, I mustn't do that. I can't.'

"'I know you want to be free of whatever it is she's got you dependent on.' I guess I'm still convinced it must be pills of *some* sort. 'But you can start over tomorrow. Today, you need to shoot this scene.'

"Sandie just sits there. 'You don't understand.'

"I stretch the telephone over, put the receiver in her hand. 'Call her.' And when she makes no movement, I take it back. 'I'll call her. What's the number?'

"'It's disconnected.'

"I can see that she's absolutely lost.

"'What's her address? I'll drive there and get what you need.'

"Five minutes later I'm running red lights with a scribbled address taped to the dash. The name that goes with the address is *Megan Kirkhope*. I toss the name around all the way out of the city and up the 101, trying to make it connect to something, but come up empty. Kirkhope's place is way up beyond Santa Barbara, and then further on still, north through the forest almost as far as Bakersfield. The house is far from being worth the drive. A shell of a place. Paint faded and scabbed. Junk on the porch. A wood pile with a litter of saw debris.

"Megan appears before I've even got out of the car. Arms folded, fingers twitching like they're wishing for a shotgun.

"'Miss Kirkhope, I'm—'

"'I know who you are. And who sent you. Just you run back to her and tell her no. Not any more.'

"So, what can I do? I'm eighteen. I don't care particularly about Sandie or even about whether the picture gets finished. I just care about making a name for myself as a guy who can get things done. So, I lie. I tell Kirkhope about how I'll be fired if I return empty handed, about my sick widowed mother, my brother in rehab, his jailbird wife and his kids in state care and already getting into trouble with the law. I lay it on like ketchup *and* mustard. When I'm done, she laughs in my face.

"'You call *that* a sob story? Try being an adopted kid discovering age nineteen that your *real* mother is every inch the Hollywood actress you'd dreamed she'd be and that she's also a wheedling, manipulative bitch who forces you to do unspeakable things for the sake of her career.'

"To say I'm surprised is an understatement. Sandie Laurence is this woman's *mother*? Kirkhope has to be older than me by at least a few years. Sandie's official studio age is thirty, but even if that's an underestimate, it can't be by much, which would have made her a mother—I'm guessing here—at twelve, thirteen at the oldest.

"Megan can see I've done the math and am already on to the supplementary questions. 'No, I *didn't* track her down to blackmail her. She found me. I'm the secret well of tears she taps into every time she has to blub on screen. Why she couldn't have left me as the lost baby of a child mother, why she had to go *further*, I don't know. But, well, here we are, fuck it all to hell.'

"She goes inside, leaves me in front of her porch trying to gauge the potential value of what I've just learned. It'll ruin Sandie's career if it comes out she has a secret adult daughter, but she's pretty much on her last chance as a viable property anyway. Hell, Kirkhope probably told me in the hope that I'll spread it around.

"She's inside five minutes, maybe ten. When she emerges again she's holding one of those grocery sacks. She hands it to me. I feel the bottle inside, liquid sloshing.

"'Tell her…' Kirkhope's been crying. 'Tell her this is the last. Tell her there's no more. It's dead.'

"'Tell her what?'

"'Tell her it's *dead*.'

"And she turns her back on me and slams the door."

Deluca looked to me for a reaction. "Well, what do you think of that?"

"That was pretty rude, I guess."

"Damn right it was rude. But that's not the end of the story."

"No?" *Not by a margin.* The carafe was barely two thirds full.

"So what happened?"

"Well, obviously I get back to LA in time to stop the crew from packing up. Sandie practically assaults me. 'Did you get it?' she says. 'Oh, you *angel*, you got it.' Then, once she's discarded the bag, even as she's glugging back the contents. 'Is this all there is?' So I tell her what Megan told me: *it's dead.*

"And right at that second everything changes. She's no longer a movie star. And I'm no longer a kid at the bottom of the studio food chain. I have power over her and we both know it. So I tell her she needs to go and do the scene now. And just like that she goes and does it. And again, she's amazing. Heart wrenching. You'd almost believe she actually had real talent all along."

"And then?"

"Well, that's it. It's a wrap and everyone breathes a huge sigh of relief and moves on with their careers. The picture does moderately well and Sandie…well, Sandie retires gracefully from the business."

"But that's not the end of the story either," I said. "What about the bottles?"

Deluca sipped his drink. Nodded, appreciative that I'd been paying attention. "Well, the water was just water, you know. Came from a local stream. Sandie claimed its purity helped her centre herself but really she used it as an excuse for contact with Megan. To sharpen up the memories and the guilt of giving up her baby. A shot of nitrous for those tears."

I waited.

"What? There has to be a *point* to the story? Son, this is true life, not the movies. Well, if there *has* to be one, I guess it's use *your advantages wisely*. See I didn't blab what I'd learned to the rags. Where would that have got me? But a quiet word in the right ear got me the right promotion at the right time. And every now and again I used it to demonstrate I understood discretion. And that, let me tell you, is a rare commodity in La-La Land." Deluca expanded in his chair then, smiled like a proper fat cat. "Son, I was a junior VP before I was twenty five."

"And as such a *paragon* of discretion, you're telling me this story now because?"

His Cheshire smile melted. "Hey, I'm passing on hard-earned wisdom here. A little gratitude?"

"That's not the reason." I placed my palm against the window, removed it. Rain ran through the fading print of my fingers the way water permeates everything. "You're telling me this now because it's raining outside and it's warm inside, and those are always the right conditions for telling stories." I nudged his whisky glass. "And you've been drinking, of course."

Deluca peered at the glass. "What do you mean? What's in there?"

I shrugged. "Just whisky. Fermented grain and water. Mostly water." The *source* of that water was another matter, but he didn't need to know about that. "But then so is everything." I lifted the carafe. It still wasn't quite full. There were two empty inches in the neck. I placed it down in front of him. In the candle's illumination the water took on a shade of darkling aquamarine, a sheen of peach. Like a sunset over the ocean.

Deluca gaped.

"The water wasn't *just* water. Tell me about what happened when you followed Megan into her house."

Deluca looked at the table top, at his glass, at his over-neat fingernails. He refused to look at the carafe, at the droplets of condensation coalescing into a burgeoning drip. But I knew he could feel the pressure of it.

"I don't want to." The words seeped from his lips.

"But you will. All stories have to be told. That's how the cycle works. You human beings. Seventy per cent water? You're all water carriers. Drinking it, using it to live, pissing it back out into the world again. Same with stories. Stories need to be consumed and absorbed and retold, distributed from speaker to listener. Even the secret ones. The deep, still water that doesn't see the light. The pure stuff. You had to know what was in those bottles, didn't you?"

Deluca looked bewildered. He'd thought he'd been telling barroom brags. Showing off with his Hollywood connections, trying to impress the cute blond waiter into after-hours drinks, a blow job in the men's room.

"You've never told anyone the whole story have you?"

He shook his head. "No one would believe it."

"You wanted to keep it for yourself." I tried not to chide. He didn't deny it anyway.

Deluca took in a thin breath, let it out through his teeth. "Megan didn't invite me in. But she didn't forbid me either. You're right, I wanted to know. I followed her inside."

He'd closed his eyes, drawn in to the memory now. His lids shivered like beetles under parchment. "I found her in the kitchen, in sunlight, rinsing a bottle in the sink. It was a Goody's green. I remember the label, that old fashioned boy's face, soaked and beginning to peel. I guessed Goody's must have been her favourite soda. She had more bottles lined up on the window sill. All the flavours. She had a stack of grocery bags too, smoothed flat on the kitchen counter. That was the kind of person she was. Thrifty but proud of it. She wasn't lying about not being a blackmailer.

"I watched her. In that light, the tap water frothing out of the overfilled bottle neck was like diamonds cascading over her hands." Deluca squinted. "Does that sound fanciful? It's how I've always thought of it."

"If that's what it looked like, then it's true."

"Megan let the water run like that, full force. It sprayed all over but she relished it. She didn't acknowledge my arrival in the kitchen, but she knew I was there.

"'Manolo came here the same day as Sandie,' she says. 'The self-same hour in fact that she arrived out of nowhere and started spewing up twenty one years of stewed guilt. I don't know if you noticed but this place is hardly on the beaten track. I don't get two visitors a season never mind the same hour. But the funny thing was, I was waiting for him. I didn't know it but I had been for a long time.'

"Megan allows the bottle to fill one final time. She towels off the outside and goes through to the adjoining room. After the bright kitchen, the parlour next door is like a cave. The lights are off, the curtains drawn. There's a smell of dust, and another smell too, a sweet-sour funk like bad milk.

"Megan is bent over a couch, and she's whispering to the occupant, helping them to sit up, to drink from the bottle. There's a sound of wet snuffles and hasty, desperate glugging. She places the emptied bottle on a side table, next to a plastic funnel and a washcloth.

"'Manolo,' she says. 'This gentleman is from my mother's movie.' The fat guy on the couch straightens up. He has dark hair that tangles in the blanket tucked up around his chin. His burnished, Hispanic skin has a sickly pallor. His wide eyes are soft like liquid chocolate. They glisten. And he wheezes when he breathes. It might be because he's out of shape or it might be because he's ill, but mostly it's because he breathes through his trunk."

The word was barely spoken. It condensed, it seemed, out of Deluca's breath. He looked to me for signs of disbelief but received only my absolute attention. Megan Kirkhope might have marvelled at the coincidence of two visitors on the same day, but there is no such thing when it comes to the stuff that stories are made of. Characters come and go, scenarios change, but everything is connected.

"A trunk." It wasn't a question. The elephant boy had a different name when I encountered him. When I distilled the story of his horrific childhood, a tale of dark solitude and silence. Of wanting, needing, someone—anyone—to communicate with. What a surprise to see him resurface like this when the very substance of *that* story was pooled in the glass by the old man's hand. A surprise, but not a coincidence.

Deluca's head bobbed shakily. "*Yes*, a proper elephant's trunk where his nose should be. With hairy pink nostrils dripping snot on the blanket before he pulls the blanket up to cover his face again.

"'Please don't stare.' Megan touches his shoulder. I think to reassure him. 'He doesn't like people to stare.'"

Deluca's laugh was arid. "Well, of course, I *try* not to, but I can't help myself, can I? He's just so fucking…"

"Weird?"

"No. *Pathetic*. I guess his whole freakish life must have been hell. He certainly seems incapable of looking after himself. Megan even has to wipe his nose for him.

"'When he arrived here we agreed to take care him,' she says. 'My mother sends money for food, but he lives with me.'

"The elephant man chooses that moment to make a sound, like a *huff*, and inclines his head angling a large ear towards Megan.

"'He wants to hear my story,' she says. But she hesitates. Then she bends to him and she hesitates again. For the longest time."

"She really didn't want to tell him."

Deluca shook his sorry head.

"She knew what was going to happen. But she had to. She blamed Sandie, but it was *her* story. And all stories have to be told when the time comes. Did you hear it?"

"No. She whispered it. Into his ear."

"What happened, Vincent?"

Deluca took a shuddering breath. It became a dry rattle in his chest. He reached for the carafe but I moved it beyond his grasp. It was almost full. He emptied his whisky glass instead. Grimaced back the last drop.

"I watched a man cry himself to death."

I waited. Let him finish it in his own time.

"So, Megan's whispering to him, and right away those big wet eyes fill up. Tears brim along his eyelids. He blinks and they start to roll down his cheeks. Without dropping a word, Megan catches them in the washcloth. That's important. She's not wiping them away; she's *catching* them, gently, like each one is a pearl. At least to begin with. The longer Megan talks, the harder Manolo cries, and soon the tears are gushing from him. Great cartoon jets, rolling rivers over his cheeks and down his trunk. He huffs and snuffles until he's hoarse and Megan's cloth is dripping. She fumbles for the bottle, wrings the cloth out into the funnel, into the bottle. This goes on. Megan whispers, Manolo cries. It's only after the third or fourth decanting that he subsides, slumps back to horizontal. Wheezing like a deflating balloon.

"Megan stops talking. She dabs the last of the tears with a mother's tenderness. Pulls the blanket up to Manolo's face, covers his trunk, covers the eyes. Then she twists the cloth to wring those last drops into the bottle. Her knuckles whiten on the rag she squeezes it so hard.

"'He's dead?' I don't know I'm going to say this before I already have. Megan flinches, but nods. 'How do you know?' I say.

"'Because I've come to the end of my story,' She takes the bottle, forces a cork into the neck. 'And so has he.' She thrusts the bottle into my hands. 'Tell her there's no more. It's dead.'"

Deluca stared at his hands.

"You didn't understand it at the time, did you?"

If he shook his head it was imperceptibly.

"But now you do. Water attracts water. Stories beget stories. It's all connected."

Deluca didn't answer. Just stared at his hands. White as dry bones and sand. I placed a beer mat over the brimming neck of the carafe and walked out of the bar.

I had somewhere new to be. A delivery to make.

A story to tell.

Neil Williamson was born in Motherwell, Scotland. He is a resident of Glasgow, Scotland. His books include: The Ephemera *(shortlisted for the British Fantasy Award)* Nova Scotia: New Scottish Speculative Fiction *(shortlisted for the World Fantasy Award) and* The Moon King *(runner-up for the BSFA award and shortlisted for the Robert Holdstrock award).*

"I've Seen Enough Hentai to Know Where this is Going"
by Chrissy Horcheimer
story by Jeff Burk

I'VE SEEN ENOUGH HENTAI TO KNOW WHERE THIS IS GOING

by Jeff Burk

[Fade in on a slutty, curvy punk chick. She is
hanging in the air, bound and held in place by vines
wrapped around her wrists and ankles.
She struggles and the vines pull tighter. The ragged
tank-top and hot-pink booty-shorts tear in her
trashing. Her tits and ass threaten to burst free.
Her green spiked Mohawk stays standing-tall.

Cut to a downward view from above the vixen.

Producer's Note: Make sure the down-shirt view of
her tits are in focus. None of that amateur shit.

The camera shifts focus and we see she is hanging
above a cavernous pit. A booming roar echoes from
the darkness.

Cut to a close up of the girl's chest as she
struggles and screams louder. Her shirt finally tears
free and her tits flop out.
Another roar and she shakes around screaming. The
camera zooms in on the jiggling.

Cut to the overhead view again.
We can see movement in the darkness beneath her. A
giant shape wells up. Massive tentacles unspool from
the black ink. The body of the beast rises up and
the giant is size of a building. Bat-like wings jut

from its back. Its head looks like an elephant but
dozens of tentacles, as thick as minivans, jut from
the obscene face.

Cut to the creature towering before the bound woman.
She trashes even harder. It looms before her, its
tentacles flick the air a few more times and then
fall limp.
The girl glances down and then shakes and screams
even louder, making sure to push out her chest so
the camera gets a good view.
The beast raises massive claws and roars, shaking
its flacid tentacles.
The woman looks down again at the limp tentacles and
her body relaxes. She stares the creature in the
eyes and looks fucking annoyed and pissed.]

"Seriously?"

"Cut! Cut!" shouts Bum Biggler from his director's chair.

"Seriously!?! Are you even looking at these tits? A faggot eunuch could get it up to these tits!" she shouted at the monster.

The beast looked down, dejected.

"Can someone get me the fuck down?" she yelled.

"Veronica, Veronica, I know, I know—" boom the director through the megaphone."

"No, you don't know! Do you have any idea how wet and lubed up I need to be to take that," she nodded to the beast's tentacles but wouldn't look at it. "My pussy is ready now. My ass is ready now. My mouth is ready now. I need a costar that is ready now."

She was lowered to the ground and interns ran up to undo her straps.

She glared at the director. "And to you, I'm Ms. Chaos."

Another intern ran up, a beefy young man wearing nothing but platform boots and a leather thong. He held out a mirror with three neatly cut lines of coke. Veronica leaned over and snorted one.

"If you need me I'll be in my trailer. Masturbating." She glared at the creature. "Someone's gotta get me off."

She stormed off the set, her sexy coke slave following closely behind.

The monster watched her go.

"Oooooo…," it moaned and the thing's tentacles dangled even limper.

He turned to the thing, "its OK big guy. It happens to the best of us. Why don't you go take ten and we'll send someone in to help you out?"

The beast shrugged, turned, and went stomping off. Each step boomed and made the whole set shake. Bum watched his other star walked off the set.

Once the thing was gone, he held up the megaphone and addressed the crew. "We don't need another fucking dud, where's the new guy?"

--o0O0o--

Life had been going pretty bad for Jacob. Truthfully, it was fucking horrible. In the past two months, his parents were killed in an airplane crash, his fiancé left him for a professional mime, his IT firm was bought out by some Saudis' and he was in the first round of lay-offs, his Xbox broke, his apartment got infested with bed bugs, and his dog ran away—he assumed out of shear disgrace and disgust over how pathetic his owner had become.

The little saving he had ran out pretty quickly and, with no one to turn to for help, Jacob had to take some drastic measures.

That's how he got into porn.

Having one's orifices ravaged by strangers wasn't the career he had in mind but it kept the lights on and his belly full, even if it did leave his asshole sore and his stomach nauseous.

He didn't have the most ripped abs or the tightest asshole but he did learn he could deep throat, better than any of his exes in fact, and that particular skill ensured he had plenty of work.

That's how he met Bum Biggler. The short, shady, Sicilian was impressed with Jacob's work and hired him to be the exclusive fluffer for Bum's films. It was better than the free-lance work he was doing before and he didn't have to worry about any family or friends seeing him in a movie (all his work was off camera).

And even though most of his work day was spent gagging on a cock, occasionally he got some perks. Like the time he went down on Wendy Wednesday for forty-five minutes. Or when he ass-fucked Barbra Bright while she checked her email (she wanted to stay loose).

So when Bum asked him to be the fluffer on his latest flick, THE DOOM THAT CUMMED ON VAGINATOWN, Jacob jumped at the chance. Veronica Chaos was the only listed star. Bum had warned Jacob that this would be one of his "specialty" pics. Meaning Veronica would most likely be sucking off pigs or sticking needles through her nipples but Jacob didn't care. She'd need someone to tongue off her cunt or ass in-between takes.

Sometimes this job had its perks indeed.

So Jacob sat in a waiting room reading an old issue of WIZARD MAGAZINE, his dick hard as he waited for Veronica.

At the far end of the room, the door popped open and a PA poked her head through.

"Jacob, we need you."

He stood up and followed her through the door. She was young, twenty at best, with small apple tits and long lean legs leading to a small, almost boy-like ass. Just how Bum liked them. And judging by her slight limp, he was living up to his name.

She led him down several halls and around a few corners until they were at a plane, unmarked door.

"The star needs you. Now." The PA punctuated the last word with a cunt turn and walked away.

His palms were sweaty and he was slightly nervous. He had seen all of Veronica's movies—TWO MACHETES ONE GIRL, FUCK ME LIKE A KLINGON, DOCTOR WHO'S IN MY ASS—all of them.

She wouldn't care about him. He knew that he would be just another face buried between her thighs, just to keep her wet enough for the next horse cock or baseball bat. But it was good enough for him.

So, dear reader, I'm sure you can understand the disappointment Jacob felt when he walked through the door.

The room was a giant dark cavern. Slime coated the floors, walls, and ceilings. Jacob could swear that he could taste it in the air—it reminded him of that old Ecto Plasma Kool-Aid. Everything seemed to be made of rock and there was no light but for some strange earthly glow emitting from above. It was if the room held its own dying sun.

It took Jacob a moment for his eyes to adjust and then he saw his client.

The thing was like a mountain in the room. Jacob thought it was some kind of strange set decoration but then it shifted and subtly rose and fell as it breathed. The thing was alive.

Was he supposed to service this?

The mass shifted toward him and he could see massive tentacles in the hazy light. He immediately knew what was expected for him and imaged them against his ass and or probing his mouth.

Sure, Jacob had blown a donkey or two in his day but this was too much.

He rushed to the door and gripped the knob. Just as he was about to throw open the door and flee and great low moan, like a whale song, came from the colossus.

He turned back and saw the tentacles from the monster lying limp. They had no desire to violate him and this was made him pause. Since he got involved in this business he had never ran into anything that didn't want to go up his ass.

"Oooooooo…" moaned the monster.

The beast looked, and sounded, sad. And, for some reason deep inside that Jacob would never truly understand, Jacob felt pity. He walked away from the door and back toward the thing.

"What's…what's wrong?" he asked as he inched closer to the creature.

His eyes had adjusted to the gloom and he could now make out what the monster looked like. It was a massive beast with an elephant like head but, instead of a trunk, numerous look octopus-like tentacles jutted forth. From its back were two colossal bat-like wings.

212

"Ooooooo…" it said again. Its shoulders slumped and the tentacles and wings hung slack.

There was a pathetic quality to the creature that spoke to Jacob. In the sadness of the thing's dinner dish sized eyes, he felt pity.

He approached the monster. Its tentacles were lying across the floor like power cables.

Jacob stroked one of the tentacles. "There. There. It's…OK."

The creature's sad eyes looked at him and then rolled away.

"Dude, don't be like that. We've all been there. Sometimes things just…don't work."

The creature sighed again, its huge bulk heaving. Jacob could tell he wasn't helping.

"There's a lot of pressure put on us. People think it's easy, why couldn't you get it up with the hotties we work with?"

The thing's eyes turned.

"But it's work. And work gets boring. Doesn't matter if you're filling pot-holes, spread-sheets, or pussy."

They both sighed.

Jacob sat down and patted the closest tentacles. "But man, fuck it, it beats a real job. Let me ask you this, would you rather be fuckin' that bitch out there or would you want to be stuck in some bullshit cubicle?"

The thing lifted its head.

"Really, this is survival," finished Jacob with his head down.

The tentacles began to twitch and Jacob stood. The thick green fleshy cables whipped around in the air.

"Glad…glad I could be of help. You go get her."

The thing made no motion to leave but instead wrapped three tentacles around Jacob. They held him tight while their tips softy caressed his back and legs.

"Ummm… yo, what's—"

A fourth tentacle slipped between his legs and Jacob's words were lost. He gasped and got hard.

The thing's touch was firm but caring and, most importantly, felt fucking good. The tip of its tentacle wrapped around Jacob's tip.

The beast's eyes met Jacob's and the thing cooed. The pleasant purring made Jacob's body vibrate and hum.

With one suave motion, one of the tentacles pulled down his pants and turned him around. Another tentacle was there for him to be bent over.

"Ohhh…" said Jacob and yet another tentacle probed at his asshole—just teasing.

This wasn't the kind of work he had hoped for but for the first time in a long time he felt truly willing, wanting.

He closed his eyes and relaxed.

BAM!

The door to the cavern slammed open. Bum Biggler stood there and looked at Jacob with his puckered asshole out and ready.

"Great job," shouted Bum. "But he needs to save it for the shoot."

Jacob looked back and saw that the monster's tentacles were now whipping through the air.

He stood and pulled up his pants.

"Alright, take five man," said Bum as Jacob walked past. He turned to the monster, "you, on set in two. We don't want to miss…" he gestured at the flicking tentacles, "this."

But before Jacob passed through the door he turned back at the beast. It was looking at him too and their eyes locked.

And they both felt a pang somewhere inside.

--oO0o--

Jacob stood to the side of the set. Watching scenes get filmed was another perk he occasionally got.

The monster was really letting Veronica Chaos have it. There was one tentacle in her mouth, pussy, and ass, with three wrapped around her waist, and yet another two coking her.

The beast pumped and Jacob watched. The thing kept his attention on thrusting and fucking and abusing Veronica but, at one brief moment, its attention was diverted. Its eyes flashed about the set and saw Jacob. For the briefest of moments the monster and

Jacob exchanged something, something that came from deep inside. Something he had not felt for a long time.

The monster pulled the tentacle out of Veronica Chaos' mouth and a hole opened on the end. Thick pure white semen, like melted marshmallow, sprayed her in the face.

Jacob felt sad.

Jeff Burk is the cult favorite author of Shatnerquake, Super Giant Monster Time, Cripple Wolf, *and* Shatnerquest. *Like the literary equivalent to a cult B-Horror movie, Burk writes violent, absurd, and funny stories about punks, monsters, gore, and trash culture. Everyone normally dies at the end.*

He is also the the Head Editor of Eraserhead Press' horror imprint, Deadite Press.

Born in the Pennsylvania backwoods, he was raised on a steady diet of Godzilla, Star Trek, *and EC Comics. He now resides in Portland, Oregon. His influences include: Sleep deprivation, comic books, drugs, magick, and kittens.*

PLEASURE SIGNALS
by Jennifer Robin

It could be said that my relationship with Michael Di Mercurio was all about experimentation. I first lured him into my world with a dream I had, one in which I was cooking an enormous pot of curry, and after consuming the curry, we had a muscular, body-quaking series of sexual feats that could only occur in a dream; the sort of sex that makes you feel that a person with whom you've had only the most casual and awkward conversation is actually an emissary from a planet where life revolves around sex; acrobatic, mystical spasming droplets of sex oozing from clockfaces, exhaust pipes, the cornerstones of buildings; we the people freed through the bondage of constitutional round-the-clock orgasm!

This dream was really a motivational factor in my getting to know Michael.

Another factor was my not-quite-ex-boyfriend Lenny. He believed Michael was mentally retarded, carried thirty sexual diseases, and was a mythical being of the woods, a feral child.

When the vegan musician you date monitors your thoughts down to scrutinizing the ingredients in your shampoo—when t*his man* calls someone a feral child, well, a feral child sounds like the *soup du jour*!

Michael really played up this feral business. He wore tattered corduroy shirts overgrown with leaf-patterns, which he paired with dirty khaki pants once marketed for business rather than for pleasure. On his feet were Converse sneakers. His hair was a mane of oily brown that cascaded to his shoulders, a hairstyle not many men in real life elected to have at the time, even though the year was 1994 and the world was seized by the mythos of grunge.

I was at a university whose resources were spent on its science programs. Straight-laced sporty-looking youth buds lined the byways between antique brick dorms. Immediately surrounding the campus was an enormous cemetery, a crack-cracked ghetto, and a diner where waitresses still called customers "Hay-unn." In the derelict industrial landscape of Rochester, New York, I felt like a dark and magnificent bird, and I wanted to meet the feral lover of my dream.

It was hot, steamy. It was summer break. I decided to stay on campus to take classes.

I loved the heat. I loved the feeling of being one of three students occupying an entire dormitory. I also loved being alone. My boyfriend Lenny graduated and moved to New York City, leaving me upstate. I had another year before I'd graduate. I was young enough that I didn't know *how* to break up. I was too young to realize that when one person moves away, this physical separation functions as a break-up, even when an *end* is not the couple's intent.

Within two weeks of moving to Manhattan, Lenny got a job doing graphic design at a time when designers were paid like kings. He holed up in an apartment in Greenwich Village, and other than going to his job, he commenced living like a shut-in. Lenny was the penultimate goth. His fear of the external world was palpable. He viewed the world in terms of predators and prey, and I was sick of feeling like *his* prey. I wanted to move on to something, or *someone*... truly unpredictable.

Michael Di Mercurio was not actually *feral*, but he had his own vocabulary. It was influenced by vast intakes of wine. Most of the time it sounded like he was saying "Hooosh-hoosh-hoosh, ush-ush-ush" until you leaned closer and could make out distinct sentences about beat poetry or blues music or tantric breathing.

Michael's day job was as a radioactive janitor. Because it was a big science university, experiments involving radioactive materials interacting with rat or monkey tissue were happening all the time, as if vivisection was going out of style. Michael would walk around with a Geiger counter to detect leaks, and somehow (I never exactly found out how) he was supposed to "contain" them.

He spent long hours in narrow supply tunnels that connected the campus to its research hospital, halls filled with a dumpster-thick heat, playing a wooden flute like a Tuvan refugee all the live-long night. As long thin streams of burned research animals were piped out of a crematorium, Michael's instrument piped beneath the earth, a sullen soliloquy.

I didn't know any of this when I invited him to eat curry with me. I thought he had wild hazel eyes, lips like rosebuds. That was *enough*.

I was fixated on my attempt to recreate *the dream*. First, I had to recreate the food:

It was 8:30. The sun had set. I was leaning over a big metal pot. I lacked basic cooking spices, so I poured a ton of spaghetti sauce and cumin and onions and heavy cream together and kept stirring. It didn't taste "dream-like" enough, so I seized a wand of aftershave-smelling incense and stirred it into the pot.

That *did* it. It was the curry of my dream.

Michael arrived, tall and muscular, coated with a sweat that could easily have been accrued by working in the foundry of Mars. His face reminded me of a deer. His eyes flashed as if they, like his name, were made of liquid mercury. While listening or observing, he often let his pillow-like lips slide apart, collecting an inoffensive yet noticeable stream of drool, such that his lips resembled those of a cherub in a Renaissance frieze.

The night progressed with us eating the curry, sitting on my bed and discussing books and the endless nothings people turn over when they have a "conversation" for the first time. Michael leaned close to my personal space—poised, expectant, waiting for me to make the moves. I felt a *rush* to have a man waiting for my command.

We drank more wine. We decided to get away from the stuffy dormitory and go to a place we both enjoyed, the cemetery. As we hopped between graves, I found ways to press into *his* personal space. I let my fingers get lost in the well-developed sinews of his upper arms. Each powerful shoulder extended from the flimsy hippie-knit vest he wore. Just touching his biceps gave me a thrill. I had never been with a man whose arms were so clearly an extension of his cock.

By 3 AM we were rolling across the roof of a mortuary engaged in an hour-long kiss. Years of wine and exertion had turned Michael's tongue into a precise piece of meat. It arched like a panther perfumed with Drum tobacco; it slithered with a salty fluidity. I dared him to take his big warm paw and pull the shirt off my chest, strike any remaining cloth from my body and drag his fingers between my breasts. The hollow of my chest felt like a pale porcelain bowl waiting to be filled with milk. I yearned for Michael to seize my heart, devour my core, and with those digits still roaming, ease lower in a line until reaching the opening between my legs, a moist cup of flesh demanding to be filled.

Michael yanked my shirt over my head. My body quivered with a cold fire. His tongue lingered at my mouth, slid into the hollow of my cheekbone. He licked a path down my jaw, his lips softening to kiss the lines of my neck. He bit my nipples with a ferocious thirst. He gripped my waist as if he was about to break me in half. His tongue returned to my mouth, inserting itself with an athletic rhythm, speaking to me of what an even lower organ would do. My hands teased the bulge in his pants where it thrust against my thigh.

I felt a pulse, hard and momentous in my groin. I didn't know it could beat stronger than my heart down there, but here—I was feeling the proof!

My entire lifetime was building to this moment: I needed Michael Di Mercurio to flood me, bite me, rip me to shreds.

--o0O0o--

Months of wine and pleasure commenced. Under the peculiar pink haze that occurs in industrial cities on summer nights, Michael and I tripped the light fantastic, shambling in and out of mausoleums, kissing on gravestones old enough to contain the parents of Ralph Waldo Emerson and his young pal, Thoreau. Smut and scum never tasted so good, being entered on the pile of clothes where Michael slept. I could press my body so close to his that it felt as though *I* was inside *him*. I came to understand the virtues of slow-motion, the magic pace that can be tasted after the slamming, the concussions and rapid thrusts. We could be joined together, barely moving at all, and the slightest twitch of my muscles over his manhood would make me slip out of comprehension into a world of radiant yellow delight.

I don't know if it was Michael's radioactivity or my general insanity, but we were well-suited to each other. For the first time in my life, I was experiencing the elusive sensation all women with our secretive parts seek: mutual orgasm.

(Fireworks; Brimstone, Lemon Zest. Every Pore Open; Every Breath a Gaze.)

By the time the school year began, our pairing was legendary. I no longer wore underwear. I flashed lampposts, park benches, and earthworms as a labor of love. I was ready to consummate my feelings with everyone and every thing. Lenny, with his pallor and his towers of precise machines, with his Oxyclean and his Tim Burton and his documentaries on animal cruelty, he would probably not recognize what I had become, which was a nymphomaniac.

Michael and I began to get followers. They would show up at Michael's apartment on the other side of the vast, palatial cemetery. Michael's apartment wasn't vast or palatial, but it was solid, wooden, cozy. His bed-nest reeked of brine. Over the months I visited him, I drew portraits of magical beings in menstrual blood above the pillows where he slept. I left an imprint on our bed; for it truly was a bed where great incantations were happening; space was traversed, barriers were broken like quarks turned into cherries, split between fine, razor-sharp teeth. No one said the words "sex magic" out loud, but followers began to show up, hoping they could join us on our tour through inner space.

Some of the followers were women with breasts and bodies so unlike mine—they had soft parts unlike my sheer bone; they had large pink aureoles to their nipples, and hair like flax. There were men, oily guttersnipe nerds with limber bodies and chaotic humor; men who stole cars and hacked ATMs as a child-hive-mind and now they were getting advanced degrees in astrophysics. I enjoyed the breezy nature of these sharp egos; I enjoyed that they knew what they wanted and didn't have to stay overtime out of guilt or misguided ideals. Inevitably there were the jealous, fish-like souls who wanted to participate, but in the end they could only take drugs in the corner and guffaw, "Geez, you two are at it again! Don't you ever stop?"

And then there was the nervous young man with a face like a halved almond, so smooth and exposed to the light. His name was Timothy Skelling. He had darker brown eyes than Michael. He had a body like a skateboarding loon. His hair was short and blonde, and his eyebrows hung over his eyes like two trellises overgrown with dying weeds. There was a look in his eyes that reminded me of a hamster peering out from the corner of a cage, uncertain: Would food be coming soon?

Timothy Skelling was the one who decided we were practitioners of a foul and demonic sex magic. He believed this to such a degree that he, when he did have a shared anthropology class with me, would duck his head in the doorway, see I was in attendance, and then dart away, literally skipping class for three weeks after the *incident* to make sure he wasn't near the vacuum-hose of my evil soul.

First of all, it should be said that Tim had a girlfriend, one of those reedy dark women who look like vanilla beans and do belly-dancing and everything that comes out of their mouths sounds like a question, an asking for permission. When Tim showed up at Michael's apartment on that dark and candle-lit night, perhaps he should have considered how his actions would look to *her* after the fact. The way it looked to me was this:

It was eleven at night. Tim had been drinking with us for a couple hours. We were listening to records. Michael had been playing Miles Davis, and then a Balinese flute piece that sounded like a morning full of rainbow-colored birds.

It was then that Michael, with his flashing eyes—oh, he had flashing eyes!—he got one of his zany looks.

Part of the rapport between Michael and I was that we were, despite our differences, both pranksters. It felt like we were commencing another prank.

Earlier in the week, Michael had found an album at a garage sale. The album's title was *Pleasure Signals*. Based on the cover art, I imagined that the music inside would be prog rock.

The cover featured an alien landscape of sand dunes, which on closer inspection were actually the breasts, abdomens, and thighs of naked women. Traversing this daunting landscape were the figures of the duo who had made the music: A guy who looked like a cross between Paul Simon and an out-of-work accountant, and a fellow with a tweed jacket who was going for the "sexy academic look"—replete with ascot and aromatic tobacco, to be sure.

Michael widened his eyes at me and said, "Shall we? Shall we? Shall we?"

His voice was low and musical. I responded by wiggling my brows and nodding solemnly. "Yes, yes. We must have the ceremony."

Upon hearing the word "ceremony," Tim looked up from his cup. "What do you guys mean...ceremony?"

I didn't know what I meant by it. I was just being funny, but Michael assumed the lead.

With his Adonis-body and his corduroy rags, Michael traipsed across the kitchen floor. He extinguished all light sources that were not flame on wax taper. He began twirling in the air and humming an esoteric tune. He turned to me and started the chant, "Plea-sure sig-nals, plea-sure sig-nals, plea-sure sig-nals."

I joined him, and we were in ecstatic unison. Michael waved his arm to Tim, where Tim was slumped against a kitchen cabinet, his rear on the dirty linoleum floor.

"Come...join us, Timothy. Come, for pleasure is to be had!"

Michael put the record on the turntable, and the air filled with a light, peppy jazz-fusion music. Having listened to plenty of prog rock years ago, I could sense that the musicians were hoping their music was sounding hard, and exotic, and full of suspense, when in fact it felt like a song that could acceptably be played in any dentist's office—even a pediatrician could depress tongues to these titty-ditties!

This is why there was even more of a sublime humor to Michael creating an altar of candles around the album's cover, right on the kitchen floor, and then getting out his largest blade.

Michael's feral "look" required him to collect and wear several blades, and this was the largest, daggery-looking blade in his collection.

He let his eyes roll back in his head, and he groaned the words, "Plea-sure sig-nals, pleaaaaa-sure sig-nals…" as he sliced, very deliberately, into the flesh halfway up his arm. He made a long slice, and the blood began to brim at the edge of the opened flesh, like an acrobat having climbed a great height before executing a death-defying leap.

Tim was drunk and stoned and his eyes were agape. I could see that he was smiling, ever so nervously, and trying to play along.

"You next, you next…" Michael handled the knife to me.

I wiped off the blade and held it above my wrist. I didn't really want to walk around for the rest of my week (or month) with a gaping wound, so I made a very small pinprick at the tip of a finger, and squeezed a drop out, to mingle with the conspicuous pool of Michael's blood already darkening the kitchen floor.

When the blade was handed to Tim, he accepted it. He made a small cut at the edge of his wrist, just small enough to squeeze out a couple drops of his own contribution. It joined the pool on the kitchen floor.

"Now…we are united…" Michael said in a trance.

The ridiculous music galloped on with bongos and triangles, awkward saxophones that never could stay on rhythm. The three of us began to caress each other and move toward the bed.

Finally! Here was something that Tim could understand.

While I didn't connect with Tim as a mind, I accepted his lean ironing-board body with pleasure. What mattered to me was the newness; a new person's touch, a new person's digits and thrusts. There was something intoxicating about seeing how the narrative would unfold. How long would it take for person 47 to lean into my personal space and initiate a kiss? Would person 52 be any good at cunnilingus? How slow, how fast? Would person 64 make me see violet stars, or would it be a tedium-fest with 64 sulking over an artisan beer and telling me stories about his unfortunate uncle's dry-cleaning business so as to sweep away the guilt of being in an orgy and losing his hard-on at the last minute?

With Michael and Tim on either side of me, I felt like I was feeding wolves and being fed by them. Two mouths were at my neck, a warm breath of wine-smoke-rubber leaking into my hair. Hands moved up and down my ribcage, getting locked in my grooves as if they might slip through my skin and grab my organs whole. I felt like I was coated in plasma, parasites. My thighs were being milked. Fingernails tore into the back of my legs, eased into the wet terminus between my buttocks, lifted me into the air.

I let Tim focus on every inch of my stomach. His tongue and hands spread across my pelvis like a stain. His fingers pressed into my vagina, easing against the sides with cautious fingernails. I felt like I was containing him, constricting myself around him. He was confused and I ate his confusion.

I moved on top of him. I felt unstoppable. I grabbed his arms and then his hips. I twirled his boy's bones and angled him to enter me. Even in the dark I could sense the shade of his sunburned skin, seeming sprayed-on and sealed beneath his dyed-yellow hair. We were dolls at shadow-play.

I sensed Michael growing forlorn. Timothy had a way of trying to ignore him. A man's body confused Tim. With each advance, the newcomer leaned away from man-meat.

At a certain point when Tim was ignoring Michael, I felt Michael get up and move into living room. He dropped the needle on the album's grooves…again. I heard his muscular feet trudge toward the altar in the kitchen.

Michael Di Mercurio moaned; he chanted; and it sounded as if he was no longer speaking English, or even his native "Whooosh-whoosh-whoosh, ush-ush-ush." I cannot say what language he was speaking in, but it was sharp, like hollow wood, predating Latin or ASCII or vaudeville swank. It smacked its toothless gums at the Romany-mother-tongue. It sniggered at New Orleans patois.

With his long lion-muscles extended, Michael stood at the altar of *Pleasure Signals*. He became an ancient root and roared.

For a moment, the piercing sound caused Timothy Skelling to get goosebumps.

I did not. I was used to Michael's attempts to de-evolve, or so I thought.

I woke up under the boughs of dry ivy that covered my ceiling. I wanted my dorm room to feel like a treehouse, but at the moment it felt more like a hospital room. Cramps filled my body with waves of pain. I was familiar with the sensation of pregnancy, and these cramps—they spoke of a fullness, they spoke of a body needing to expel a mass; a tumor, a too-much.

I got used to shadows. In bright sun, I frequently saw my body cast two, or sometimes three versions of me. I got used to waking with what sounded like a hundred voices in my head.

I decided to rationalize this as part of my brain's development. Surely there was a reason my brain, usually at dawn and at dusk, felt like an old-fashioned telephone operator's switchboard. I heard so many conversations; some were mundane, women's voices talking about soccer matches, or pumpkin pie recipes, or complicated medical procedures I had never heard of, like colitis, and blastocystis hominis, not to be mistaken for the grits.

When I felt the sensation of tongues in my ear, I would tentatively press a finger to my ear canal. There was no drool, no tongue.

I saw less of Michael for a few weeks, perhaps because of my pain. Like me, he became difficult to get a hold of, and when I did catch him on the phone, he sounded more drunk than usual. Instead of being able to decipher the words within his "Whooosh-whoosh-whoosh, ush-ush-ush" it really *did* just sound like *whooosh-whoosh-whoosh, ush-ush-ush.*

One morning I woke at 6:53 AM from a dream where I watched the sun, looking a lurid peach color, rise and awkwardly set. It moved back and forth over the horizon as if it couldn't make up its mind whether to go all the way down. I watched a second sun creep up behind the first sun. It appeared to be teasing the original star. It was trying to force the original sun off-course.

I felt a great emptiness inside the second sun. Was it a sun, or was this a clever disguise? Its identity was beyond my understanding of biological life. It was so old, so calloused, of an order of intelligence I could not begin to describe.

When I awoke from this dream, the presence of the second sun remained with me. I stared intently at the objects in my room, trying to remember their names, trying to remember my own name. It was difficult. My life didn't seem *real* compared to the second sun.

I spoke to the room as calmly as possible: "Who are you…and what is it you want?"

No answer.

It was a cold day in spring. The cramps were making me feel colder. Despite the pain and the class-work I needed to finish, I bundled up and walked through the cemetery to get to the other side where Michael's apartment was. I needed to see him in person and tell him what was happening to me.

The door was unlocked. I entered, passing the curtain covered in daisies, passing the silver candlestick holder, passing a doodle made in my blood.

A smell like sour milk and rusted metal filled my nose.

The record—for what *other* could it be?—was playing on the turntable, though at this point the sound was marred by pops and scratches; disjointed areas where it seemed that the needle might rise of its own accord to escape the damaged grooves.

The album cover had been moved to a place of prominence on the oven. Melted wax nearly obscured the original cover art, the imagery of those goonish musicians jumping on the "dunes." A sun was about to set over the enormous breasts, the engorged flesh, but hovering behind this first sun a second shape appeared. As I stepped closer, I saw that the shape was a hole in the cardboard with a scorched black corona, as if a cigarette had been repeatedly pressed into the cover.

It stared at me, like a black eyeball. I felt the gravity in my body change: It was the *second sun*.

I stepped around the patterns of blood on the floor. There were never complete lines or strokes, so much as wild *drips* that made a Rorschach on the linoleum and ancient dusty wood.

I followed the scent to the bed.

Michael was sitting there. His body—was sitting there.

Something that I once would call Michael was sitting upright, and covered in a membrane that appeared to be made of wet newspaper. I could barely distinguish the features of his face under the membrane; however I could feel the *second sun*, the black sun, more intense than ever. It held residence in this room. It was pulling me toward the bed.

The body of Michael began to turn its head in my direction.

It felt like hours, but was probably only minutes, as I repeated the word "nothing" in my head, and backed out of the bedroom, out of the kitchen. I tried to focus my way through the last few feet before the back door, past the winter coats on hooks smelling of onions and man-sweat, and into the cold green aridity of spring.

As soon as I eased through the side door, I broke into a sprint. I ran until I had no more strength in my legs.

Nothing…nothing…nothing… I repeated as I felt my heart start to slow five blocks away.

The cemetery never felt so *peaceful!* I walked back to campus outside the cemetery gates, staying close to the flow of dumb-animal-traffic.

When I returned to my dorm room the pain in my guts was worse than ever. I ran to the bathroom and liquid came out of me—out of one hole; out of both holes—dark, oily, like something left in a parking lot with a black Trans-am racing away.

My body, it was trying to expel something.

"I have to figure out what to do. Okay, okay…" I whispered to the bathroom stall.

I was shivering. I felt I had touched something that would fill me with its nothing-nothing-nothing if I lingered near it.

I stood under a dormitory shower, hot water getting snagged in my lips, my forehead pressed to the cool green tile. I wanted to be clean.

While I lay under a blanket in my room, I could feel Michael on the other side of the cemetery. Was I imagining him there, or was I *feeling* him there?

I wondered if I should protect myself. Was I really free? I had just emptied myself. I didn't want to be filled again. I could not go back.

The phone beeped. The answering machine turned on. Lenny's nasal voice was piping to me, telling me about his life in New York, seeming to scold me for having not called him in three weeks. He called me a pet name, "Pumpkin-cheeks." Lenny still believed that there could be something *to us*.

For the rest of the day I sought company. I sought stupidity and hot cocoa in the big glass-roofed school Commons, a five-story megalopolis shaped like an alien crack rock. As I watched buzzing groups of people discussing voting procedures and facial piercings, I kept asking myself if I should have taken the needle off the record…

But no, all I could do was get *out* of there! Only to spend weeks, months, years after this wondering if I was really safe.

Jennifer Robin lives and dies in Portland, Oregon. She writes grotesque prose about the Zonked Checker, The Crack Whore Morton Salt Girl, and drone strikes by the simple syrup. Her first novel, Bouzi, *was published in 2000. Her poems and short stories have appeared in* PLAZM Media, Dark Bizarra, Whole Beast Rag, *and* Unshod Quills. *Her autobiographical book of essays and surreal street sketches,* Death Confetti, *will be released by Feral House in 2016.*

Is This How it Feels to Fall in Love Again
by Anna Suarez

Rebirth is loud on city streets.
In the language of love and daffodils,
You take in the scent of my thigh,
And I'm not shy tonight,

So I look at you.

I walk home
Before the air chills,
Count the azaleas
On the trees

And cry.

Last night I associated your presence
with morning rain and bluejays, then
pulled the red sheets over my head,
melted into satin

monde rouge.

What if I whispered Fear
Instead of Joy,
Choosing
Montmartre, Marseilles,
Over le desir de minuit:Breath/Breath,
Hands/hands, behind a lace curtain.

Tenderness has always smelled
Of fear & spring dew.
Intimacy,
The flutter inside the knees,
Drops of rain on goosebumps,
Somewhere beyond the tumult,
Grandiose waves of
Dreams and Indecision
I want you, somewhere beyond
My eyes closing with your weight,

I want you.

ARTISTS' BIOS

Robert Branaman *is a film-maker and painter from the US.*

Veronica Chaos *is an x-rated ventriloquist who spends her time making people uncomfortable on the Internet.*

Louis Fitch *is a Chicago based photographer in the burlesque scene.*

Chrissy Horchheimer *is an artist living in Portland. Her art has appeared on the cover and interior of* Super Giant Monster Time *by Jeff Burk as well is books by Carlton Mellick III, Kevin L Donihe, Edward Lee and many others.*

Annie Sprinkle *is a former adult film actress, an erotica writer, a sex educator and a champion of human sexual expression in all its form. Alongside her partner Elizabeth Stevens, she has created and spearheaded the ecosexuality movement.*

ND - #0440 - 270225 - C8 - 229/152/20 - PB - 9781907133916 - Matt Lamination